Helping your

FOCUS ON THE FAMILY®

Helping your Child Succeed in Public School

Cheri Fuller

Tyndale House Publishers, Wheaton, Illinois

HELPING YOUR CHILD SUCCEED IN PUBLIC SCHOOL

Fuller, Cheri.
Helping your child succeed in public school / by Cheri Fuller.
p. cm.
ISBN 1-56179-709-X
1. Home and school—United States. 2. Education—United States—Parent participation. 3. Parent-teacher relationships—United States I. Title.
LC225.3.F84
370.19'31' 0973—dc20 92-20857
CIP

A Focus on the Family book published by Tyndale House Publishers, Wheaton, Illinois.

Editors: Nancy Reynolds
JoAnne Sekowsky
Larry Weeden

Cover design: Al Eiland

Printed in the United States of America

99 00 01 02 03 04 / 10 9 8 7 6 5 4 3

It is to Flo Perkins, a dear prayer supporter, and to the Christian parents, children, and teachers all across this country who are truly salt and light in their schools and communities, that this book is dedicated.

Contents

Acknowledgments

I want to thank those people who have helped to bring this updated version of *Helping Your Child Succeed in Public School* to life: Larry Weeden, my skillful editor; Perry Glanzer, Focus on the Family Education Policy Analyst, for his excellent research and insights on current educational issues; Beth Weeden, for her public school experience and suggestions; Judy Hoffman, for her consulting and contributions on character education; and especially Marilyn Olson, without whom the final revisions wouldn't have been typed!

My appreciation also goes to Fern Nichols, Jeff Myers, Karen Gale, Wendy Flint, Posy and Tom Lough, Carolyn Curtis, Melanie Hemry, Peggy Stewart, Teresa Caraway, Susan Gainer, Carl Rehberg, Mary Lippert, and the many parents who allowed me to hear and share their experiences.

And always, thanks to my agent, Greg Johnson; my supportive and precious husband, Holmes; and our three children, Justin, Chris, and Alison, who have taught us so much in their educational journeys and growing up years.

Introduction

As I complete this updated version of *Helping Your Child Succeed in Public School,* I am more convinced than ever of the tremendous need for parents to be proactively involved and in fervent prayer for their children and their schools.

Since the original book came out in 1994, some things have changed in public schools: There are more charter and enterprise schools, and thus more possibilities for parental choice. Some of the controversy over "OBE," or outcomes-based education (which now exists in U.S. schools under more than 30 different labels), has been replaced by controversy over school-to-work (a rearrangement of the traditional curriculum, starting in primary grades, to integrate career awareness and leading to students' having to choose a "career pathway" by seventh grade).[1] Sadly, violence in our schools has increased, as in the recent tragedy at Columbine High School in Colorado, and thousands of kids now bring weapons to school each year. The Internet plays a far bigger part in the education and life of most students, both in the classroom and on the home front. Many parents can now log on and receive classroom updates and homework suggestions from their child's teacher via E-mail.

But a few things haven't changed, except perhaps to increase in importance. One is the need for you to know your child's teachers and build a working relationship with them. Another is to know what your child is being "fed" academically and what the textbooks and teachers say about science, history, sex, and other subjects. And more than ever, you need to provide regular prayer cover for your child and his school, make sure your child learns to read and write and compute competently, deal with problems when they arise, and become a part of the decision-making processes at the school.

Why? Because no one can replace *you* in the education of your child. Professional educators don't entirely hold the key to children's success at school or to the improvement of schools. Parents are vital. Current studies continue to confirm that parents and peers, not teachers, have the greatest influence on students' performance.[2] And when parents join hands and work together, they can have a great impact on the schools their kids attend. Parent groups in Wisconsin raised academic standards throughout the state. Parent groups in New Jersey started new, public charter schools to provide a higher quality of education. Parents in Tennessee got a "safe sex" curriculum replaced by an abstinence-based program. Parents in California got educators to adopt better reading programs that were phonics-based.

For a number of years, I have spoken to and worked with parents and teachers in public, private Christian, and home schools. I have a great love and respect for children and families in all three educational environments and a desire to help unlock the incredible potential God has created in each child. I do that by motivating and equipping those with the responsibility to bring out the best in them, their parents and teachers.

I believe God directs parents who seek His will into the schooling options that He knows are best for their children and families. For some, that means Christian or other private education. For a growing number, He directs them into home schooling. But the majority of Christian children in America are still enrolled in public schools, where their parents face special challenges. I've tried to address many of those in this book, in part through the new chapters on school choices, character education, and computers at home and school. In addition, the appendixes at the back of the book have been updated with information about all kinds of abstinence-based sex education programs, books, videos, and organizations that help support public-school families. My hope is that the resources provided here will be a great encouragement and a source of practical assistance.

Please note, however, that though this book is geared to parents whose children are in public schools, it's also useful to parents whose children are in parochial or other private schools. All parents need to relate to teachers, deal with those problems that inevitably come up, help their children with reading, writing, math, and science, guide them in getting organized (unless you have one of those intuitive organizer/studious kids!), and help them study for tests. Most Christian parents also want to develop their children's characters, grow their faith, and pray for them.

From my vantage point and my contact with schools in different parts of the country, and especially with moms across America who volunteer for, undergird, and assist teachers, praying not just for their own kids but also for others in their schools and baking cookies and driving endless carpool hours—there is reason for hope and not despair, even though many schools still have huge problems.

While Congress still debates the legality of prayer in schools, tens of thousands of Christian children and teenagers pray on their public-school campuses. Thousands lead prayer clubs and Bible studies. Most of these student groups sprang up after 1990, when the Supreme Court upheld the constitutionality of the 1984 Equal Access Act that required public high schools to permit student-led religious meetings if other extracurricular clubs could meet on campus.

In addition, I'm tremendously encouraged by the Moms In Touch, International groups praying weekly for public schools—more than 25,000 groups in the U.S. alone, and thousands more throughout the world. Their U.S. goal is that by the year 2003, every single school will be covered by a group of praying mothers who regularly intercede for the children, teachers, and principal. Hundreds of teacher prayer groups have begun as well through the Christian Educators Association, which encourages teachers and administrators to make their classrooms "lighthouses of prayer."

As all these groups pray, God is working: Principals and teachers are coming to Christ; bridges are being built between parents and faculties; more Christians are getting involved as volunteers and decision-makers; and new abstinence-based sex education programs have started.

In many districts, character education programs are building values in school children, and released time programs, where public-school students receive biblical instruction during the school day, are increasing.

While these and many other positive strides are being made, however, much remains to be done. And more than anything else, prayer is our greatest influence and best hope for change. We can work and volunteer, serve on committees, and seek to be a Christlike witness in our children's schools, but we can't change hearts. Only God, through His Spirit, can transform hearts and minds, bringing a spiritual awakening to America and turning the educators who write curriculum to truth instead of the prevailing postmodern, secular philosophy that has shaped much of what we now see in America's public schools.

Perhaps we can learn a lesson from Nehemiah, who, while in Babylon serving as the king's cupbearer, heard news of the devastation of Jerusalem—that the city walls were broken down, the gates burned, and the remnant of God's people left in affliction and despair. He was terribly grieved at the condition his people were in, somewhat like what we feel when we hear about drug problems or violence in youth or see the problems in our local public schools. Our nation's moral walls are broken down, and we see the results in our children and schools, whereas theirs was an actual wall.

In response to what he heard, Nehemiah wept, mourned, and fasted for days, calling on God in prayer. He also took action. With the king's permission, Nehemiah went back to Jerusalem to lead the rebuilding of the wall. And while directing that work, he prayed all the way and encouraged the people to turn their hearts to the Lord. In fact, in the short autobiographical book of Nehemiah, he prayed 11 times.

Many of you will set out or are already working to "rebuild the walls" in your local schools or community. But more than that, you want to see others return to God as Nehemiah did, and you're praying up a storm. What happens when God's people not only act but also pray? God moves. We see this countless times in the Bible. And in Nehemiah's case, the prayer and action resulted in the wall's being rebuilt and the city restored against terrible odds and formidable enemies in only 52 days. Many of the people returned to God's Word and ways, but they still faced big problems. And Nehemiah continued to pray to his Lord, lead, and work as God directed.

Over and over in situations today, we are seeing the power of united prayer and action and are realizing that when we pray for our schools and our children, nothing is too hard for God. An atheistic principal of a California public school came to Christ after being prayed for by three different Moms In Touch groups, and now he influences administrators throughout his San Diego school district. High schools previously riddled by gangs, drugs, and alcohol have become places where young people's lives are transformed by Jesus' love, where safety and peace now reign so learning can be the focus.

Another example of the power of parental prayer is what has happened in an Oklahoma school district in recent years. For some time, one lone Christian on the school board stood up against the tide of trends and values that she felt would be damaging to students. Suffering defeat after defeat in board votes, she told parents and a prayer group at her church, "We've got to rebuild the walls just like Nehemiah and return to God's ways, and it will only happen through prayer."

Teachers in the district who saw firsthand the negative impact of curricula and policies on students also asked Christian parents to get involved and, especially, to pray. And as more and more parents did just that, they began to see results. Within two years, two additional believers were elected to the school board.

Finally, in the spring of 1999, the tide had turned completely as a fourth Christian, in a landslide victory, was added to the board. Shortly thereafter, the very liberal school superintendent resigned. The parents and these Christian board members know there's much work still to do and that it will take time, but they're in it for the long haul, and they continue to pray that God will show them how to shape a public educational system based on godly principles.

Like Nehemiah, we've got to mix prayer with all we're doing to rebuild our schools. We can pray for salvation for every student, teacher, and administrator as we drive up to the school to tutor a child or deliver treats for a class party. We can pray for our children's feet to stay on God's path as we wash their sweatshirts. We can pray about textbooks, volunteer to serve on textbook and curriculum committees, and seek the Lord's wisdom to develop the best character education programs possible. And as we work and gather to pray with other parents in agreement for our children, schools, and leaders, dynamic things will happen to bring about renewed hearts and lives—beginning with our own. Our schools—even our states and nation—can be changed. As Oswald Chambers said, "A praying saint performs far more havoc among the unseen forces of darkness than we have the slightest notion of."

CHAPTER 1

Does Parent Involvement Make a Difference?

Joel charged into the kitchen, threw his books on the table, and cried, "I just can't do this."

Before Earl and Peggy Stewart moved their family of five to Oklahoma City, their children had either been home schooled or had attended private Christian schools. But because they could no longer afford private school, all the children were now attending public school. The two older boys were adapting well, but it was Joel, their sixth grader, who was their greatest concern.

Joel's elementary years had been tough even though he was in a small Christian school. He struggled academically throughout fourth and fifth grades. Now going into sixth, his standardized test scores in math totaled only 15 out of 100 and 27 on language.

How could a child facing these learning difficulties cope in a new public school and much larger classroom?

Here he was after only one week of school, throwing his books on the kitchen table and giving up.

His words catapulted Peggy into action. Maybe she didn't have the money for private school, but she did know how to pray. She had prayed many times in the past about Joel's learning problems. She knew that somehow, in some way, God would lead her to a solution.

Peggy's answer came in volunteering in Joel's classroom. By being in the classroom each week, she got to know his teachers, was able to see what they expected of him, and how to make the most of the materials they were teaching. She got supplemental materials for him, sheets such as "Reteaching Long Division," and she and Joel worked together on them every day after school. If his assignment was math, they did half of the problems together and he did the rest himself. Peggy would check his work, and Joel would rework the problems until he understood what he was doing. They made flashcards so he could practice his spelling words each week, and they often read aloud the science and history textbook pages, using a globe, atlas, and extra books to enliven the material.

That fall Joel entered the science fair. After a family brainstorming session, he decided his project would be on the variation of heat energy absorbed by different colors. The whole family helped gather materials, supported him, and cheered him on as he worked. They all shared his joy when he took first place in his division. Joel, who had always been overshadowed by his high-achieving older brothers, felt his confidence rise.

After his achievement at the science fair, and with the help of caring teachers and support at home, Joel began to *double* his study efforts. He decided to "go for the gold" and earn straight A's. By the fourth nine-week period, he did it! For the first time in his life, he made all A's! But the most improvement was in his standardized test scores: They rose *40 to 50 points* by the end of the year. Joel's total math battery rose from *15 to* 98 and total language from *27 to* 89!

His parents' involvement and the support of his teachers helped Joel develop confidence. He began to know that "I can do it! I can be an achiever." Joel persevered through high school and college. As a junior and senior, he was a consistent straight-A student and on the President's Honor Roll. Recently he was also inducted into an honorary academic fraternity and chosen for a selective Christian honor society and the student alumni board. More than anything, Joel loves to learn and wants to attend law school. That's quite a set of achievements for a boy who struggled with his homework in sixth grade!

YOUR CHILD'S EDUCATION: WHOSE RESPONSIBILITY?

We all want to see our children succeed in school, whether they go to Christian, private, or public schools. I'm happy to say that Joel's story is not an unusual one. While I was researching and interviewing people for this book, I saw over and over again that the bottom line to your child's success in school is *parent involvement*. We know from looking at more than 50 research studies that when parents get involved in school, those schools improve dramatically; their children are more motivated and better behaved in the classroom; their diverse needs are met more effectively; and scores on achievement tests are significantly higher.[1]

Moreover, those parents I interviewed who are actively connected to the school had children and teens who were not just surviving but excelling academically, maintaining their values, and growing in their faith. These parents are building bridges between the home and the school so they can better carry out their responsibilities as parents and secure the very best education for their children.

Such parents consider their child's education as *their own personal responsibility*—not the school's. They see teachers and other school personnel as helpers in meeting educational goals for their children. Public school may be where their children obtain part of their education, but the parents provide additional academic enrichment opportunities for the children.

My husband, Holmes, is a builder. Wise parents build relationships with teachers much as Holmes does with his subcontractors (the framers, trim carpenters, plumbers, etc.). When he designs and builds a house, Holmes meets with them and goes over the plans. At this point he gets their input and lets them know his expectations for their craftsmanship. They continue to communicate regularly with each other. Often while the work is in progress, they meet at the housing site. If there are problems, they figure out the cause and come up with solutions. But the ultimate responsibility and liability for building the house rests with the builder, for he is the "general contractor." In a similar way, parents are the directors or general contractors of their child's education. They're in it long term, from kindergarten through college. The child may have many teachers along the way, but his parents are his primary instructors and guides. Parents "sub-out" parts of the educating task, but they must oversee, provide support and resources, take the initiative to keep in touch, and hold school personnel accountable for their part of the project. These parents roll up their sleeves and help whenever possible. They know one teacher can't possibly do the myriad tasks required and still meet the diverse needs of all the students.

"Although Allison spends part of her day in a Washington state public school," said parent Bill Mattox, "my wife and I believe we are her most important teachers. It is we, not the principal and teachers, who are ultimately responsible for her education. It is we who will be held accountable to God." Even though their school district had an all-day kindergarten program, the Mattoxes felt that attending kindergarten only in the mornings was best for Allison. The school cooperated with their goals for that year, and this arrangement gave Allison more time for lots of reading at home and outings, and her parents were able to take advantage of the teachable moments in everyday life.

SALT AND LIGHT

The parents I interviewed had diverse reasons for choosing public school. Some chose because of finances, others because of location and community situations. Still others because their child had a handicap that required special education programs not available in their local Christian schools. But many parents felt a strong sense of *calling* and *mission* to place their children in public school. "To us it isn't which school option has the least amount of problems or the most to offer our children, but what does God want for us and which school system has He equipped us for," said another parent, Carolyn Curtis. Since she and her husband, Carl, had backgrounds in public schools and Campus Crusade for Christ, they felt equipped to handle any problems they might encounter in the schools. They also made a careful choice about the community to live in and the school system available in that area. They have been able to keep their children in public schools and accomplish their goals for them. Every year they re-evaluate their situation.

"Carl and I believe the Bible says that we should live in the world and not retreat from the marketplace (Acts 17:17, 1 Peter 2). We're supposed to be light, and light is most needed in the dark, in the business world, and in the public schools," said Carolyn. "Carl is light in the business world, and the children and I are light in the public schools. We feel we're equipped to be survivors in these places, and we're equipping our children to be survivors, too."

"Byron and I feel God has called us to be in the world and not of it," said Lin Smith, a California mom. "We're to be salt and light where God places us. We believe the family is a divine institution to share Christ in the community around us. If we're not a part of society—PTA, youth soccer, the local women's club, school—how can we be salt and light?"

"I believe Christian kids and families in the public schools are the compass that points to true north, a moral North Star," says Jay Abramson, a Connecticut dad. "If we all pull out, others won't know which way to go. We *must* be there to point in the right direction."

When Jay and his wife, Liz, moved to a different state and their sons entered the public schools, it wasn't easy. "Kids gave our seventh grader a hard time," Jay explained. "They told him he dressed funny and wasn't wanted there."

As in the Abramsons' case, there are always problems to be solved, but if our children can stay in public school and become strong, they will stand true when they go to college and on into the business world. "It's a little like subjecting plants to mild frosts in the fall to 'harden them off,' " Jay explained.

Hardening off a plant (by protecting it with a tarp or cloud cover spray to keep the frost off) makes it strong enough to survive cold winters and hot summers. The plant is thoroughly watered to insulate and protect the roots. If a plant doesn't have this slow acclimatization and is hit by a hard frost, its growth can be stunted.

This "hardening off" process reminded me of what other parents shared about how they equipped, prepared, and supported their children—through the prayer cover (like the tarp or cloud cover spray), their involvement in the classroom, and their teaching values at home (regular watering that insulates the roots). There are real dangers of the frost that you have to be aware of. "You can't assume that the school represents your values or that they support the idea that there is absolute truth at all," said Jay. "That's why we've got to dialogue regularly with our kids and make our voices known at school." None of the parents I talked to denied there were problems; rather, several said, "We want God to use us in the lion's den; there's much work to be done."

LET'S NOT GENERALIZE

One day I was on my way home from teaching creative writing workshops for children in a public elementary school near our city. I thought about how blessed I had been by the many Christian children, Christian parents, and committed teachers I had met while working in this school the past few weeks.

My thoughts were interrupted by a guest on a radio program who was generalizing about how bad every public school in America was and that you would never want to send your children there to be educated.

Though well-intentioned, he repeated a familiar negative theme throughout his discussion. I'd heard these generalizations before, and I knew they weren't entirely true. Yes, there are many public schools that have problems—lots of them. But I thought of the schools I had been in that year that were good places for children to learn because of the involvement, prayers, and commitment of parents, as well as the quality of the teachers and principals in the educational process.

I thought of the many Christian teachers in public schools and young people in our church, some of the strongest Christians I know, who attend many different public schools. I was reminded of the parents who prayed for God's guidance and felt led to put their children in the local school in their town and then get involved in that school.

If you decide that God is calling you to do this, first of all, it's important to note that public schools vary from town to town and state to state. Most schools tend to reflect the values of the people who live in a particular community and their commitment to education.

One local public school staff may be respectful of parents' authority, reflect conservative values, and welcome your involvement. Another district may have a more top-heavy bureaucracy, be run by people who don't share your values, and are resistant to your involvement. You can't generalize because each school is different. Although many Christian parents opt for religious schools and home schooling, the majority of all children from American Christian homes are in public schools.

HEROES OF THE FAITH

One of the blessings of conducting research for this book has been meeting and talking with parents from all over the country. As I heard their stories and situations, I began to see them as true heroes of the faith. Like you and me, they are busy with jobs, household responsibilities, and stresses in their lives. They are all in mission fields, and some are in battlegrounds. They face difficulties, but I am inspired not only by their commitment to Christ and their own children, but also to the other children, families, and teachers associated with the school. I'm humbled by their dependence on God and their sacrifices. Some give up second incomes so moms can be active volunteers at school and available when the kids come home. Both working dads and moms give of themselves to serve on textbook committees, send notes of encouragement to teachers, come to conferences, lead after-school activities, schedule times to help in the lunchrooms, and help their kids with homework.

I'm encouraged by the diligent prayers of the hundreds of Moms in Touch[2] groups all over the country, and by the many, many amazing answers to prayer. I'm touched by their faith in action.

"I trust God, but I don't have to sit at home and blindly think everything will go okay," said Judy Hartsock, a mother in Norman, Oklahoma. "There are so many things I can do! I haven't found any path yet where there have been closed doors!"

Parents like Judy, Jay Abramson, Lin Smith, Carolyn Curtis, Paul Heath, and many others I interviewed across the country, are having a tremendous impact. They are lighting candles instead of cursing the darkness.

- Parents are spearheading reading and writing projects; others are doing research on sex education and developing abstinence-based curricula for their school or district.
- Parents are introducing character education and helping to get Fellowship of Christian Athletes or Released Time Christian Education started in their school.
- Parents are having their businesses sponsor or "adopt" their child's school, adding funds and community support to the school's efforts.

- Parents are mentoring at-risk kids to give them a better start.
- Parents are beginning or leading parent associations to get other parents involved.

In the following chapters you'll read about their creative ways of working in the schools, how they are making a positive difference, how they are equipping their children, and getting their needs met.

I'm thankful to have met these parents and to have heard what God is doing in their lives, their children's lives, and their schools. As you read this book, I hope you'll enjoy meeting them, too, and will gain the practical help we gleaned together. I hope you'll be encouraged, as I am, that God is working in public schools all over the nation through Christian parents, children, teachers, and principals!

If you have chosen public education for your child, my prayer is that this book will enable you to:

- help your child make the very most out of school.
- help you build a working relationship with teachers.
- build foundations at home that will support your children emotionally, spiritually, and academically, so they can do more than just survive public school—they can succeed and grow into a generation of champions.

And I hope through the stories of these parents you'll know how much *you* matter and how *you* can make a difference in your child's education.

In addition to covering broad issues, such as how to get involved, how to deal with textbook issues, and how to handle problems that arise, you'll also find lots of nuts-and-bolts suggestions for helping your child have a great public school experience.

Whatever your reason is for putting your child in public school, he can succeed, grow stronger in his faith, and get the necessary preparation for life. This book shows you how to make that happen.

CHAPTER 2

Choosing the Right School for Your Child

"Where is my child going to attend school?" That's a question all parents face when their child has his fifth birthday and is ready for kindergarten. Actually, they probably consider the matter long before that milestone! They also have to make school choices when the family moves to a different city or a child is ready to move on to middle school or high school. Sometimes they have to consider a different school because the present one isn't working or the child has needs that can't be met there.

In any case, becoming informed about what schools are available in your area and their programs, educational philosophies, and approaches is a key step in helping your child succeed academically.

One of the heartening trends in public education today is

that more school choices are available to parents and students than ever before. There are Edison, for-profit schools, classical academies, and charter schools of different kinds. And with the expansion in school choice, more than ever you need to evaluate a school to see if it fits your child's needs. Although there's no perfect school this side of heaven, your chances of choosing the right place for your child will improve greatly if you do some "homework" (i.e., talking to parents, school board members, students, and teachers) and pray, pray, pray. In addition, consider the factors and questions listed below. You've got to look beyond the glowing reports in a video or brochure on the school.

The first step is to consider your child's needs, such as where the schools are located (which may affect his ability to participate in after-school activities, etc.); whether your child has learning disabilities or special needs; whether your child has a talent for music, art, or math that needs nurturing; whether your child learns best in a structured environment or in a more open classroom situation; and so on. Then make an appointment to visit the school, interview the principal, and meet the teachers. As you do, remember that the principal is the key to much of the atmosphere and priorities of the school, and that the teachers are the key to what goes on in the classroom.

Here is a more complete list of factors to consider and discuss before choosing a school:

- Does your child need the greater attention available in a smaller class? Would he do better in a large- or small-population school?
- How close to home is the school you're considering?
- Does your child need special education?

- What are the implications for after-school help, extracurricular activities, and so on?
- What are the expectations for student achievement? The best schools have faculty that require excellent work and exemplary conduct and that boost children's desire to learn.
- Is an emphasis placed on instruction and on a strong academic core of courses, where the goal is mastery in reading, writing skills, math skills, and so on? Do teachers use a variety of teaching methods to ensure that all students learn?
- Does this school have well-trained teachers and adequate facilities and funds to meet your child's educational needs?
- Is student progress assessed regularly? If there is grouping by ability, do students have opportunity to move *up* in the groups, and what does it take? Will your child receive sufficient attention?
- Does the school seem to be efficient and well-run?
- *Crucial:* Is parental involvement encouraged and appreciated? What's the principal's and the school's general attitude toward such involvement? Besides asking the principal about this, also ask parents in the community whose children have attended the school. Although some aspects of parental engagement are determined by the school board, each school's openness is determined mainly by the principal and teachers in a particular school.
- Do parents serve on school improvement committees and on curriculum/textbook or library committees, along with faculty and administrators?
- Look at the school's volunteer program. Does it even have one, and if so, how active is it? Do parent volunteers work with students and teachers in the classroom and other areas

of the school instead of just acting as room mothers and fund-raisers? What does the parent organization do, and how active is it?

- What are the school-wide policies?
- What values are reinforced by the school? For instance, is there a sense that cheating is wrong and honesty is valued? Look at the school's statement of mission and goals. What does it reflect about the school's moral values? Do those values harmonize with your educational and moral values and what you want to teach your child?
- What are the discipline procedures, and what reward system encourages the behavior of those students who achieve, are responsible, and behave well?
- What safety precautions does the school take regarding weapons or potential violence? For instance, what are the consequences if a child brings a weapon to school?
- What are the outcomes, or goals, for the school, by grade? Are they academic or attitude/behavior/feeling-based?
- Can parents request an individual teacher that they feel would be best for their child's learning needs?
- Do the principal, counselor, and teachers show a positive attitude toward students and parents? Is the principal a Christian? What about the faculty? Do school personnel show respect for students? Do teachers assist those who need special help, motivate those who don't care, and discipline those who need to gain self-control?
- Are school pride and school spirit evident?
- Are bright students challenged? For example, can students accelerate and take the next level of math if they have mastered their grade level? Are there advanced placement

courses for gifted high school students?

- Look at the school library. Good schools have good libraries staffed by a media specialist or librarian.
- What percentage of graduates from the high school go on to college?
- What's the drop-out rate? What are the SAT scores, and have they declined or risen in the last five years?
- Is the sex education program abstinence-based or value-free? What kind of drug-and-alcohol-prevention and/or AIDS-education curriculum, videos, and instruction are offered? Can parents ask that their children be opted out of these programs if they conflict with their moral or religious beliefs?
- If you have a child with learning problems or handicaps, consider how the school handles such students. Is speech or occupational therapy available? Are special-needs kids mainstreamed in the regular classroom or put in a separate class?

The pro's of mainstreaming for part or all of the school day (which is called "inclusion") include: good role-modeling and benefit from interaction with regular classmates; boost to self-esteem if the resources are provided so the special-needs child can experience success, learn effectively, and feel like a regular kid; challenge and stimulating activities. The cons of mainstreaming include: lack of one-on-one help (if there aren't enough personnel to provide an aide with the child in the regular classroom); the child may need more direction and help than can be offered in the regular classroom; inability to participate fully; and absence of "safe" surroundings since the child isn't in the protected environment of the special ed classroom.

In a separate classroom, there may be more one-on-one instruction, more opportunity to participate, a smaller class size, and a more protected environment. As you weigh the pro's and cons, looking at your goals for your child, you can decide if those goals can best be met in the special ed classroom, the regular classroom, or a combination of the two. And at IEP (Individual Education Plan) meetings before the year starts, you can get the input of the school and work with teachers to make sure the resources your child needs are available.

- What music, orchestra, and band programs are available? What other extracurricular programs are offered to help kids discover talents and make friends?
- Look at a sample report card and any other assessment of students. One midwestern school listed a category of "Connectings" rather than grades. Do you need to be a psychologist to read the report card?
- Ask the state department of education for a "school profile" that lists class size, student-teacher ratios, student test scores, the percentage of graduates entering four-year colleges (for high schools), and other helpful information.
- Most importantly, *visit the school or schools you're considering during a regular school day (before you enroll your child)*. Tour the facilities. Sit in on and observe a few classes (especially in the grade your child would be attending and the next grade level). Talk to other parents. Note class size, order, and discipline in the classroom. If you will have a student going into the middle school or high school in a short time (one to three years), look at the schools your child will be attending in a few years.

As you evaluate schools, clarify your priorities. And ask God to show you what kind of schooling option would be best for your family.

EXPANDING SCHOOL CHOICE

A group of 17 parents met recently to organize a new charter school (an independent, publicly funded school designed and run by a group of business leaders, educators, or parents) in the northwest suburbs of Boston. This particular charter-school group consisted of soccer moms, a doctor, engineers, a karate teacher, a computer whiz, and an attorney. All had been heavily involved in their children's schools as classroom volunteers, parent-teacher organization leaders, or committee members. But the more they saw of existing public education, the more they wanted something different for their children. With an ambitious goal of providing a rigorous, fact-based, traditional education emphasizing cultural literacy and moral character, North Bridge parents applied for one of the 12 school charters to be issued in the state of Massachusetts. Their school planned to open during 1999.

Mary Lippert, an Oklahoma City mom, had first gotten involved in her child's elementary school as a classroom volunteer and a parent-teacher organization leader. But as her son neared middle school, she wanted to have more influence on the curriculum and overall education than was available at local schools, and she began to hear about a group of parents and educators working on the design for a new middle school—an "enterprise school."

Even though the Oklahoma legislature had failed to pass charter school legislation, the city school district had passed an "enterprise school policy" in July 1997. Enterprise schools don't qualify for federal funds set aside for charter schools, but they grant the same annual per-student allotment as other schools receive. "Enterprise" means a contract between the school district and other parties—parents, teachers, or business leaders—to create and operate schools for the purpose of improving student achievement and increasing learning opportunities for district students. Like charter schools, enterprise schools have site-based management and the autonomy to hire principals and teachers, decide what curriculum and textbooks to use, and so on.

When the Oklahoma City School Board adopted this policy, the door opened to outside groups to take over site management of schools tasked on a written application, administrative review, and board approval. Mary and the other parents in a group called the Committee for a Neighborhood Middle School at Belle Isle-Burbank Campuses filed their application on sites for a District 2 middle school that would open for 150 sixth-graders in the fall of 1998 and grow one grade at a time to reach full enrollment of 450 in the fall of 2000. After appearing before the board of education three times, they received an enterprise school contract in April 1998.

The enterprise committee invited parents, community members, middle school teachers, middle school counselors, and middle school principals to contribute to the decisions made concerning: type of curriculum and level of academics (they chose the E. D. Hirsch Core Knowledge Curriculum Sequence), foreign languages to be studied (Spanish, French, and Latin were chosen), electives to be offered, whether uniforms should be required, and textbook choices.

Since Mary became the curriculum committee chair and they didn't have to choose books on the State Adopted Textbook List but could use what would fit their sequence and objectives, she had a great time pouring over history, science, English, and math texts. She did research at a university library and at textbook depositories, and she also looked at various private school texts. She and the other committee members used the Hillsdale Academy resource guide they had purchased as well, plus home-school catalogues, to find the best books available.

The parents wanted a school with high academic standards, so they established an admission requirement that students score in at least the 70th percentile on the Iowa Test of Basic Skills (ITBS)—which means students must score higher than 70 percent of all the students tested nationwide—or have a B average. They also instituted a uniform policy, an honor code, and a behavior contract between the students and the school.

Guided by the Core Knowledge Curriculum Sequence of E.D. Hirsch, the students follow a block scheduling format that includes math, science, social studies, language arts, P.E., art, Spanish or Latin or French, music (in the form of band, strings, or vocal music), computer, library, and study hall. To that the school added extracurricular activities such as German club, Odyssey of the Mind, journalism club, sailing, and basketball.

"The most important aspect in the founding of the school is the Lord's hand in all of this," says Mary. "There has been a lot of stress, but also a great amount of peace about what we were doing. People would come up and say they were praying for us. Things just fell into place, and obstacles were overcome. When we met with the principal for one of our planning sessions, she said she had prayed about her decision to be a part of our school and she was sure it was God's plan for her. We have also found that our teachers are committed Christians active in their own churches. We know these are the kind of people we want teaching our children."

Like the North Bridge parents and the enterprise school committee in Oklahoma City, parents all over the country are seeking better educational options for their kids—and are willing to be part of the solution. And more than ever before, a variety of legislative proposals is expanding parental choice, giving hope and opportunity even for low-income families and students in inner-city areas. Some merely expand choice within the public system, and some expand choice beyond it. Let's look at a few of the most common options:

Intradistrict or Interdistrict Choice. Under intradistrict choice plans, parents and students may select public schools from *within* their own district as long as there are openings in their preferred school. Eleven states allow public school choice within some or all districts.[1] With interdistrict choice, parents and students may choose public schools from *beyond* their district as long as there are openings. And 18 states currently have open-enrollment laws that allow the choice of public schools throughout the state.[2]

Postsecondary Options. These programs allow high school students (usually juniors and seniors) to take all or part of their course work at a public—and in some cases, private—college or university within the state. Currently, 12 states have comprehensive postsecondary-enrollment options that pay all or the majority of course costs and allow the credits to be applied toward both secondary and postsecondary schools.[3] Seven states allow students to take college courses but require the students to pay tuition costs.[4] Iowa pays for the courses, but the law restricts the credit to secondary schools.[5]

Charter School Legislation. Charter schools are publicly funded schools authorized to operate semi-autonomously from state and district regulations. The number of charter schools has risen rapidly since the first one in St. Paul, Minnesota, in 1992 to more than 1,200 operating in 27 states and the District of Columbia.

In most cases, the schools can be created by parents, teachers, or community members around a specific educational philosophy. As a result, they allow parents a larger degree of control over their children's schooling. Those directing the charter school make important choices about curriculum and other facets of school life. Although they're financed by the same funds public schools usually receive, charter schools are exempt from some bureaucratic rules and restrictions and have the freedom to hire and fire teachers, principal, and other staff. They also are held to a high degree of accountability (since students choose to attend rather than having to attend because they're in a certain location).

At the time of this writing, 34 states and the District of Columbia have charter laws.[6] There are different types of charter schools. For example, in one district in Colorado Springs, Colorado, parents can pick from several choices:

Classical Academy is funded by the district but is autonomous, its board of directors made up of parents who make decisions under approval by the district board. Parents have much control and make many of the key decisions. The Classical Academy emphasizes "back to basics," teaching phonics, classic literature, Latin, and so on.

Edison is a for-profit school run by the Edison Company under the umbrella of the district board. The Edison school day is normally two hours longer and the school year lasts an extra six weeks. Placing a big emphasis on technology, every student gets a computer, both at home and at school. Parents can review their child's progress, communicate with teachers, and E-mail other parents via the computer.

Edison schools are part of a nationwide chain of privately managed schools aiming to revitalize American public education. The individual districts pay Edison a certain amount per child per year, and if Edison educates students for less money, they can pocket the difference as profit.

Edison schools are not the only for-profit schools operating in the U.S. Aramark, a private corporation, last year opened 28 for-profit elementary schools in eight states and is planning to open more in the years ahead.

International Baccalaureate (IB) is an extremely academic, very tough school requiring a lot of homework. It can be a standalone school or operate as a "school within a school" at the elementary, middle, or high school level. The IB is an international program that follows the same curriculum and standards as the state but uses a different method of teaching called the "Inquiry System" and acclimates a student to attending school overseas. The diploma is internationally recognized and can reduce college course requirements. There's a half hour of French every day for all grades, kindergarten to grade five, and an optional immersion program where the student takes half the day's studies in English and the other half completely in French.

Those are just a few of the many kinds of charter schools. Educational philosophies vary widely, from back-to-basics and core-curriculum to technology-based, to interdisciplinary, project-based learning. For example, at the New Country School near Northfield, Minnesota, active learning and projects are used for instruction rather than worksheets and lectures, and there's one computer for every two students. Since charter schools have to provide their own facilities, New Country meets for classes in a downtown storefront facility and is smaller than the average school, with 95 students in grades six through 12.

Another school, Hickman Charter School in northern California, has 550 students, kindergarten through eighth grade. They combine public- and home-schooling methods, and students do all or most of their work at home, with class instruction at six school sites. The Hickman school designs its own curriculum rather than use packaged or commercial materials.

O'Farrell Community School in San Diego is a charter middle school with 1,400 sixth- through eighth-graders. Teachers work individually with students in a project-oriented approach, and the student population is broken into "families" of approximately 150 students each to provide a sense of community. O'Farrell is housed in a building that was formerly a public school.

Expanded Home-Schooling Options. Currently, all 50 states allow home schooling. However, some home-schooling parents would like to send their children to select public-school classes or activities. Laws that would permit home-schoolers to participate in a wide range of public-school activities, from attending classes on core subjects to extracurricular or interscholastic activities such as sports and band, would give parents greater choice in directing their children's education. Currently, nine states have specific legislation allowing parents to home school their children in some subjects and send their kids to public school for other core classes.[7]

Tax Credits and Deductions. One of the best ways to achieve greater justice in educational funding is through legislation that allows tax credits and/or deductions to parents for educational expenses such as tuition and books. The tax breaks apply to all parents but are especially helpful for those parents who chose *nongovernmental* educational options. Furthermore, tax credits and deductions avoid unnecessary church-state entanglement because the benefits are given directly to the parents and not the schools. Tax deductions that don't favor one particular educational option have already been declared constitutional by the Supreme Court (*Mueller v. Allen*, 1983). In addition, an education tax credit program in Iowa was declared constitutional by a lower federal court (*Luthems v. Bair*, 1992). Such tax credits or deductions could help low- and middle-income families make educational choices.

Private Scholarship Programs and Tax Credits. Recently, a number of private voucher programs (cash stipends that can be used to pay private-school tuition) have sprung up in dozens of different cities to meet the needs of low-income children.[8] One helpful legislative proposal would grant a tax credit to individuals who make contributions to a 501(c)3 charity that gives 90 percent of its funds for scholarships to low-income children wishing to attend private schools.[9] Such a piece of legislation recently passed in Arizona, giving a tax credit of up to $500 to individuals making such contributions. And in 30 or more cities, funding for vouchers is provided by private donations so that low-income children can attend independent schools, both secular and parochial.

Vouchers. State-funded vouchers, operating on the same principle as the G.I. Bill, give parents a particular amount per child that can be applied to the cost of a religious or secular private school. Voucher programs that only allow use at secular schools are found in New Hampshire and Maine. Programs that provide vouchers for students to attend secular private schools and parochial or religious schools exist in Milwaukee and Cleveland. Moreover, the Milwaukee program was recently declared constitutional by the Wisconsin Supreme Court. And even as I write this, the Florida legislature has just passed the first statewide voucher program that allows parents to choose public, parochial, or other private schools for their children when their current public schools have been deemed inadequate.

NO NEED TO SETTLE

With parents starting reform groups like those that develop charter schools and task forces to create change in their neighborhood schools, with the expanding options available, and with all the factors to consider in finding the right school for your child—it's clear that the old days of passive parental involvement are gone. You don't have to settle for a one-size-fits-all school or a low-quality education for your child. By being informed and involved, you can have a big influence on your child's education, beginning with your choice of school.

CHAPTER 3

Getting Your Child's Needs Met in the Classroom

Kerry is a talkative, red-haired eight-year-old. She works diligently at her desk for a few minutes, then spins around to see how her friend Terri is doing on the assignment. Across the room, shy, sensitive Brian works alone quietly. In the back row, Kim, wearing a look of complete frustration, shuffles and reshuffles worksheets. In the front row, center aisle, sits John. He has stuffed his half-completed worksheets into the desk and is busy flipping his pencil. Next to John is Ryan, who has already finished his work and looks bored.

Each of these children has special needs. Kerry needs structure and careful explanation of new concepts. Brian needs someone to assure him, to boost his confidence, and to encourage him to interact with other students. Kim has an auditory processing problem. She needs extra help and a seat toward the front of the room. John is the class live wire and has difficulty concentrating. Ryan needs to be more challenged. So many needs, and we've only talked about a few of the children in this third-grade class!

In today's crowded classrooms, one teacher may have more than 25 students, each with varying emotional, physical, and mental needs. How can you ensure that your child's needs are met at school? How can you know what is expected of your child, keep lines of communication open, and be aware of the different needs of the average, the learning disabled, and the academically talented student?

KNOW WHAT IS EXPECTED OF YOUR CHILD

"When should Daniel learn to add and subtract, multiply and divide?

"How can I know if Sherrie is reading as well as she should?"

"How well should my child be writing in third grade?"

Knowing what school personnel expect your child to learn during an academic year is one of the first steps toward meeting his needs in the classroom and preventing problems.

For example, third-graders are expected to memorize multiplication and division facts through 12 x 12; recognize equivalent fractions; understand the use of letters in simple algebraic statements (ab = 12); and learn estimating and rounding-off skills.

In language arts, third-graders learn to use conventional spelling, punctuation, and capitalization to write stories; learn how to identify character, plot, and setting in stories; and improve reading comprehension. In social studies, they learn historical facts about their state and country, begin to learn geography, and study maps.

If you know that certain math skills must be mastered, that a certain level of reading ability must be reached, or that certain writing skills must be learned, then you'll be able to help your child progress on course and get help if necessary. If there's a problem, if he's falling behind, you can ask the teacher how to encourage him and help him improve the deficient skills at home.

Rick von Kleist, a California principal and dad, gives each parent a list of the child's grade-level expectations at the first parent-teacher meeting of the school year. "Parents need to know the goals their child should be working toward," says Rick.

If your school doesn't provide such a list, ask the teacher for a "Grade Level Expectations" sheet that explains the academic goals in math, reading, language skills, social studies, and science for a particular grade level. Once you have a list of the academic goals, you can watch your child's progress. You can reinforce what he is learning by encouraging him to use math in the grocery store, do special projects, play board games, and read. (See chapters 9, 10, and 11 for many ways to help your child learn.)

In addition, find out about your child's daily class schedule. What subjects will be covered? Are there certain days when he must complete worksheets? When are his quizzes and tests? How much homework is given? How long should it take him to do the work?

MONITORING HOMEWORK

Another way to help your child learn the required skills is to help him with homework in the evening. Although you need to be involved, you should not do your child's homework for him. Parents' function is to monitor homework, support the child, answer questions, and help only when needed.

If the daily classwork papers Carson Caraway brings home from school show he has a problem with math, his mom, Teresa, a speech pathologist, watches for homework assignments and makes it a point to help him with them. She tries to discover what he doesn't understand; she spends extra time helping him with problems; and she tries to help him grasp multiplication or division concepts. She also watches for practical situations where math can be used around the house. For example, she gives Carson and her other son notepads and says, "Okay, boys, we need apples today. They are 69 cents a pound. If we need two-and-a-half pounds, how much are we going to spend?"

Valerie is both a mom and a teacher. She tells us, "I read over my daughter Kelsey's work and we discuss it. If she's already gone to bed, I write her a note on a yellow sticky that says something like, 'I appreciate your work on this' or 'What a lot of effort you put into this report! Good job!' or 'Maybe we need to practice this together.' "

Kelsey goes to a big school with classes of more than 30 children. It would be easy for her teacher to overlook her and any problems she might be having. However, even though Valerie is a full-time working mother, she doesn't wait until a problem becomes serious. She watches the daily classwork, and if Kelsey's grades drop, Valerie immediately talks to the teacher, asking, "Are there problems? What can I do to help?"

Watch for opportunities to communicate with your child about his school experiences. The car ride home from school or snack time after school provide chances for parents and children to discuss the school day. You can also make school and what your children are learning part of family dinnertime conversations.

MEETING THE NEEDS OF THE AVERAGE LEARNER

In public schools, there is a tremendous need for the average learner to be more challenged. One educator observed that public schools may do a good job with the academic superstars and the educationally or physically handicapped, but the average child can fall through the cracks of the system and just drift. "The greatest virtue of average students is that they don't cause trouble," said a principal, "but it is this virtue that also causes them to be ignored. These 'middle-of-the-roaders' are often expected to work on their own while the overworked teacher focuses on bright kids, those with learning problems, and troublemakers."

In most schools, as students approach eighth grade, they are tracked into low, high, and average classes for math, English, and science. Then in high school, they enter corresponding tracks, such as remedial, vocational, general, academic, or honors.

Stanford University professor Dr. Sanford Dornbusch says that 85 percent of all students finish in the track in which they started as ninth-graders. It is *very difficult* for average- and lower-track students to change tracks since schools often make decisions based on past rather than present performance or on improvement. Honor students often have the best teachers and educational opportunities. Thus, the child in the middle may be slighted. Parents can help this situation by finding ways to challenge their students—no matter what their IQ or standardized test scores.

Parents are often unaware that there are different educational tracks. However, they need to become familiar with the system. Find out what courses your student is taking and what track he's on. He needs you to be his advocate. Dr. Dornbusch advises, "You want your child in the *highest track* in which she can perform. If your child has been in average-track English, maybe it's time to say to the school, 'Look, why don't we give Sarah a try in Honors English for three to six months?' Usually the school will comply with a trial period. Then it's time for you and your child to get to work. Get the student some assistance: tutoring, much encouragement, and anything to help her catch up with the higher track."

Even if the student cannot change to higher-track classes right away, at least he or she could occasionally participate in the more demanding classes. Sitting in on discussions and debates and doing research on an area of interest, challenges and encourages the average-achiever.

If students *are* grouped according to ability, make sure that just because of a low reading score, your child is not placed in the low group in science, math, etc. Dr. Arnold Burron recommends, "Let school personnel know that you expect different grouping standards for different subjects . . . All children do not fit into one mold. Programs, expectations, and materials must be individualized to bring out the best in each child."[1]

Cooperative learning, where an average-achieving child is paired with a brighter child for science lab work or a history project, might be helpful. A mentorship program in which a student works with an adult professional in a field of the student's interest also inspires and challenges students.

MEETING THE NEEDS OF SPECIAL STUDENTS

Some children may have problems communicating, processing information, or learning to read. Other children have physical handicaps. Parents need to be especially involved with the school to address these needs.

The federal law states that learning disabled or handicapped children must receive education to meet their particular needs and that parents must be involved in planning the individualized program for their child. In addition to the many programs, there are trained people in the communities, as well as in the schools, to help these children. Parents need to seek out these resources and implement the best plan for their child's development.

The Individualized Education Plan (IEP), a blueprint of special helps designed for an individual child, aids parents of special education students. First, the child's capabilities, level of achievement, and skills are determined by his test scores, and his needs both at school and at home are considered. Then a conference is held with parents, teachers, resource specialists, counselors, and a speech therapist to design the IEP. Sometimes the child is included in this meeting.

Jason, the eighth-grade son of Debbie, a Tulsa, Oklahoma, mom, has a significant hearing loss. When he entered a junior high school of more than 2,000 students, he was to be mainstreamed into regular classes. Before school started, Debbie set up a meeting of resource people to discuss Jason's needs and the program that would be best for him.

After speech evaluation was completed, it was decided that one day a week Jason would work at speech therapy articulation and miss one section of an elective class. He would sit in the front in all his classes, and his teachers would do a quarterly evaluation, in addition to the regular grading periods. Each teacher would record Jason's progress to keep his parents informed.

Don't give in right away to a teacher who calls your child a slow learner. Once a child is labeled "learning disabled," it is almost

Caution: *If your child needs extra help, find a tutor or do it yourself. If your child has learning differences, has a learning problem, or is a late bloomer, don't let him be given a negative label. Labels can stick and damage your child's view of himself and his ability to learn. They also lower the expectations of those around him.*

impossible to get him off the slow track, even if he makes progress or the problem is corrected.

A University of Virginia education professor who tutors elementary kids said she finds that the vast majority of "learning disabilities" are problems that could be solved through one-on-one instruction. For example, a second-grader was labeled "learning disabled" by her teacher because she failed consistently at adding columns of two-digit numbers. The child's mother didn't believe or accept the label. When she watched her child do homework and add 35 to 35 to get 88, she realized the child had been adding *across* instead of up and down. Because the mother discovered the problem, the label was removed, and the student was able to stay in the regular math classroom.

If your child needs extra help, find a tutor or do it yourself. Perhaps you know a retired teacher in your church or a college student who would be willing to tutor. The extra help and attention often boosts the child's confidence, efforts, and skills tremendously. It is further encouraging to him if he can stay in his regular classroom and learn to compensate or overcome a difficulty.

Katherine Newman's nine-year-old daughter Angela had a learning disability that caused her to have difficulty staying on track and focusing on written work for any length of time. "By all rights and with her difficulties, Angela should have had a disastrous school experience," said Katherine. "But it's been very good. Because I've been active in her classroom, giving individual reading help to students and transporting kids on field trips, I've known how to help Angela at home." Angela's teacher is likely to say, "There's a problem in this area, but you can work on this at home." Trust has been built between Katherine and the teacher because of her participation in the classroom.

Helping Your Special Education Child Succeed in School

When evaluated at age two, Susan Gainer's son Joshua had an IQ of 50. His parents were told he would probably never walk, talk, or have a normal life. "No hope," the doctor said. Joshua did not speak until he was six years old. But through the prayers, patience, and dedication of his parents and Susan's work with the school, Joshua (now 18) reads at a 10th grade level; his vocabulary is post-college level; and he has never made below a C in a regular class. He is in regular ninth-grade classes except for math, has friends, and is responsible and organized.

The difficulties Susan faced with her child may be different from your struggles, but I wanted to share what she has learned from guiding her special son through 14 years of public education.

Susan's Suggestions for Helping a Special Education Child

- Keep all testing results, records, and conference notes in a file at home in order to track your child's progressive development.
- Claim your rights as parents to access your child's academic file. Don't allow a school to keep records from you. A child's academic history can play a considerable role in his course placement. Before Susan's children changed schools and districts, she removed the records she felt would prejudice testing in the new school and kept them for further reference.
- Set goals slightly beyond your child's capability. If he fails, lower the expectations to a level where he can succeed. "However, I found with my own child that he never failed, and we were continually setting new, higher goals," Susan said. "I see many learning disabled and special education

students who are not challenged because parents and professionals do not want to 'frustrate the child.' They are given meaningless grades for just putting forth minimum effort. No one knows what potential these children have because they have never been asked to work. They need to experience failure and overcome obstacles. Your child may need to work twice as hard to make a C, but the character it builds equips him to function as an adult in a world that will not make accommodations for him in the workplace."

- Have regular conferences.
  1. Make an appointment the first week of school for a conference with all your child's teachers. Let them know you are going to request their observations of your child's progress and behavior.
  2. Have at least one conference per grading period. Susan also receives Joshua's weekly report that contains his grade average, behavior evaluation, and notification of missing assignments.
  3. Write down all your questions as well as any new information that you feel would be helpful to the teacher before you go to the conference.
  4. Take notes during the conference that you can refer to at following conferences.
  5. Listen to the teachers. They have valuable input that you need but may not want to hear; give them the benefit of the doubt. Go home and think about their comments before you react to or make a decision about what you've heard.
  6. Assume your child's teachers are trying to do the best for your child. An adversarial approach cannot

build the kind of partner relationship your child needs you to have with his teacher.

7. Encourage teachers to call as soon as a problem arises and show appreciation for their help. Bad habits and difficulties need to be dealt with immediately to avoid creating a pattern.

- Volunteer wherever help is needed: Work in the lunchroom, bring cookies to PTA meetings, tutor other students. It's good for your child to see you there. Special children often have social difficulties. Being at school as a volunteer enables you to observe your child's social skills. Don't be angry if other children don't help him; they are only children and often make immature decisions.
- Consider difficulties as blessings. Look to God for hope.
- Respond objectively when another student hurts your child. "I always try to ask myself, 'Is this a situation that any other child would encounter in the course of growing up?' " said Susan. "If so, you can thank God that your child was included in the normal mainstream of life. You can discuss appropriate responses with him. However, if there is a physical threat to the child or if he has been singled out for group ridicule, inform the school personnel so those responsible can be watched."
- Give the child a daily homework assignment sheet that the teacher will complete. The child must take the responsibility for picking it up after class, bringing home the necessary worksheets, maps, books, etc., and giving the sheet back to the teacher at the first class the next day. Have a set routine and work place for homework. As soon as your child comes home, ask for the assignment sheet

and necessary materials. If he has forgotten something, you will still have time to drive back to school to get it. Let him have a snack and time to play outside after school. After his playtime, he needs to start his homework.

- Don't ask the school to be responsible for your child. There may be things the school cannot do because of lack of funds and personnel. *You* can help by giving of your time, by praying, and by being available to both your child and his teacher.
- Act on behalf of your child. A parent may find it necessary to confront school personnel about an area in which the school has failed to fulfill a clearly recognized educational responsibility. In that event, be firm but not hostile. If you absolutely cannot resolve the situation, consider removing your child from that particular school setting. However, this action should be taken *only* as a last resort.
- Praise and encourage your child's hard work and have fun with him!

MEETING THE NEEDS OF BRIGHT AND TALENTED CHILDREN

Some children are several grade levels ahead of their classmates and score high on standardized tests. Academically talented students may become bored in the classroom. Except for an occasional "enrichment time," they often receive little stimulation from the curriculum and few opportunities for intellectual challenges.

"Generally, we don't feel our son Kyser is challenged at school," says Posy Lough, a home-business mom. "So our aim is to surround him with opportunities at home. We love learning and thankfully, he does too. We encourage him to be diligent with schoolwork and find resources, books, and activities to enrich and challenge him."

Parents working with the school and the teacher can help meet a bright child's needs. "If your superachiever is bored, ask the teacher to enrich the curriculum or offer special projects," says principal Rick von Kleist. "Let the teacher know you'll be glad to do part of the legwork needed for these projects."

Parents can challenge their gifted students in a number of ways at home. Parents and children can work on special projects together, go to museums, keep an observation log, investigate animals at the zoo (many zoos have learning programs for kids with a special interest in animals), or participate in space programs at local planetariums or children's museums.

The *Junior Great Books Program* offers another avenue of enrichment within the school. The program includes a series of 12 readings per year from the second through 12th grades as well as training for parents, teachers, and program leaders. Parent volunteers can conduct book discussions during lunch or after school. Rather than focusing on fact questions, discussions should utilize higher level thinking skills. The children test generalizations, share ideas, and develop socially and emotionally.[2]

Parents can also enrich academic opportunities with some creativity and fund-raising. One parent I know saw the lack of hands-on science materials, lab equipment, and resources for a quality science program at her child's school. After presenting the needs to the parent organization, she got funds designated from the annual spring carnival for science and volunteered to research the best resources for their money. By the next fall, the students had new materials and were off to a year of discovery in science learning. If music, foreign language, or art programs are lacking, parents can join forces to find qualified volunteers from the community or among the parents themselves to teach these courses. The more parents are involved in planning, curricular decisions, and all phases of enrichment at school, the better the education will be.

IDEAS FOR DEVELOPING YOUR CHILD'S GIFTS AND TALENTS

There are so many ways you can help your child develop his gifts both at home and in the community! God has given every child special talents and gifts, and opportunities must be given to develop them. Your child may be spatially talented, have interpersonal or intrapersonal gifts, or have musical or kinesthetic talent.

Talents and Gifts

Linguistic Intelligence: Skill with words is characterized by fascination with word play from an early age. This child is very vocal and loves to tell stories.

Logical-Mathematical Intelligence: The ability to reason and solve mathematical problems is characterized by early computation skill, curiosity, and the ability to think visually.

Musical Intelligence: Ability with the sounds and rhythm of music is seen in children who at a young age can imitate tone, rhythm, and melody, remember songs from hearing only once, and love to sing and make music.

Spatial Ability: Children with spatial ability can naturally visualize an object in their mind's eye and even imagine how it would look if it were turned around. They love to make interesting designs and illustrations.

Bodily-Kinesthetic Intelligence: The child who has this gift has the ability to coordinate his muscle movements, operate with grace and timing, and use his body and other objects with skill. His precision, power, and speed make him a standout in athletics, dance, drama, and mechanics.

Interpersonal Intelligence: Children with interpersonal intelligence have great "people skills" even from an early age, an understanding of others, and an ability to lead. Sociable and friendly, they place a high priority on friendships.

Intrapersonal Intelligence: This gift involves knowing one's own feelings and abilities, and being introspective and opinionated at an early age.

These gifts may not be nurtured by the school. For instance, if your child has a visual/spatial gift, art classes would be a good addition to his schedule. However, recent budget cuts in school art programs may require you to develop his talent outside the classroom.

The following list suggests activities to develop various talents.[3] The gifts are given in parentheses following the activity idea.

- Join a "read-and-discuss" group. Libraries have story hour, drama workshops, demonstrations, discussion groups, and chess clubs. (Linguistic, Interpersonal, Logical-Mathematical)
- Plant a garden. Your child can be responsible for a small garden by planting seeds, buying plants, tending the garden, and harvesting the crop. (Logical-Mathematical, Kinesthetic)
- Volunteer at a nursing home. Children can play instruments, sing, read to residents, do puppet shows, and interview and record the residents' life stories. (Musical, Interpersonal, Linguistic)
- Attend the symphony, concerts, and musical performances in your community. Play classical music at home and

encourage children to play the piano or another instrument. Sing together as a family. (Musical)

- Learn crafts. Give your child opportunities to learn woodworking, cross-stitch, calligraphy, knitting, etc. (Visual, Kinesthetic)
- Find an art class for your child and give her opportunities to use her talent. Community centers, craft shops, and art museums offer art lessons for children. Children talented in art can make posters for school and church events, or even create a felt Christmas banner. They can frame and display their creations. (Spatial/Visual, Kinesthetic)
- Volunteer at the library shelving books and reading to toddlers. A middle-school or older child who is an excellent reader can read stories or make tapes for the blind. He could also volunteer to read to children at a child-care center. (Linguistic, Interpersonal, Intrapersonal)
- Teach your child to use a compass. (Logical-Mathematical, Kinesthetic)
- Learn a foreign language. Tom Lough's company is headquartered in Denmark, and many Danish people visit them, bringing tapes and books. They also have Christmas songs in both Danish and German, and Tom recently bought his son a child's German dictionary. (Linguistic, Interpersonal, Intrapersonal, Musical)
- Read encyclopedias together. Parents can browse through an encyclopedia with their child. Together they can discover and discuss new information. (Logical-Mathematical, Linguistic, Intrapersonal)
- Give your child a disposable camera for picture-taking on your next trip. After the photos are developed, he can

arrange them in a scrapbook and write captions under each one. (Visual/Spatial, Kinesthetic, Linguistic)

- Go on family outings and field trips. Visit the bread factory, pet shop, nature park, zoo, horse stable, downtown business district, museum, living history farm, grocery store, fire station, or any "behind the scenes" places. (All intelligences)
- Provide construction sets, building blocks, small wooden logs, and other building materials. Browse through garage sales for objects to take apart, such as old clocks. (Kinesthetic, Logical-Mathematical, Visual/Spatial)
- Supply drawing materials. Provide clay, paint, markers, watercolors and scraps of fabric, yarn, and other materials. Frame your child's masterpieces. (Visual/Spatial, Kinesthetic)
- Provide math puzzle books that involve problem-solving and strategy. Play games such as chess, Battleship, and Pente. (Logical-Mathematical)
- Explore the possibilities for learning enrichment that a home computer can offer. Try out computer math games, desktop publishing, graphic arts, architectural design, music composition, and much more.

In the next chapter, we will look at the powerful impact a teacher has on your child's learning and how to develop a good student-teacher relationship.

CHAPTER 4

Forming a Good Student-Teacher Connection

After parents and family members, teachers have the *greatest influence* on the lives of children. Research shows that children achieve more in school when they have positive relationships with their teachers.

Recall a teacher to whom you felt close; often you'll discover that that teacher taught you the most. I vividly remember my first-grade teacher at Robert E. Lee Elementary School in Dallas, Texas. Her name was Julia Rogers, and she had a contagious enthusiasm for learning. She recognized that each of her students learned differently. When I finished my assignments early, she would let me help her by decorating the bulletin boards or assisting another student.

The bond she formed with each member of her class, not just

me, was so strong that Miss Rogers went on with us to the second grade. Later she invited all of us to her wedding (I still have the pictures). Miss Rogers influenced my whole view of learning and my decision to become a teacher.

A good student-teacher relationship brings many benefits. "The students who talk with teachers about upcoming projects or what they are covering in class have an advantage and do better on tests," says Marilyn Morgan, a Dallas, Texas, sixth-grade teacher.

Students who have good relationships with their teachers feel comfortable about asking questions in class or about coming to see them after school. Especially in high school, where subjects are departmentalized, students excel more if they can discuss their subjects with their teachers. The teacher can identify and solve a student's problems before they become overwhelming.

Positive student-teacher relationships inspire students to go beyond the basic classroom requirements, develop their talents, set goals, and seek career direction. Teacher-author Guy Doud observes that teachers are truly the "molders of dreams" for their students.[1] Many people credit a teacher's inspiration and encouragement for their own successes.

John, a sophomore new to a large high school, was encouraged by his speech teacher to compete in speech contests. He won the two qualifying rounds and then competed at the state level. Because of his teacher's influence, he auditioned for a play and was chosen for a lead part. He continued taking drama and speech throughout high school. He now plans to become a lawyer, a career that draws on these high school experiences.

The benefits of a healthy student-teacher relationship are numerous, but the relationship itself requires work. Let's look at qualities of a good teacher and how to find a match for your child.

CHARACTERISTICS OF GOOD TEACHERS

The teacher's personality, values, and style significantly impact our children's learning. In his excellent book *Helping Kids Cope: A Parent's Guide to Stress Management*, Dr. Arnold Burron says:

> As a professional educator with over a quarter of a century of experience, I am convinced that the single, most important factor in a child's education is the belief system and the personality of his teacher. It is far more important than the teacher's education, the physical environment of the school, the quality of the materials, the social structure of the classroom, or any other education-oriented factor. This does not mean, of course, that other factors are not important; obviously, a delightfully gregarious illiterate, holding classes on penmanship out on the open range of the windswept plains near Douglas, Wyoming, would not be a wise choice as a reading teacher for a first grader. It does mean, though, that parents should be vitally concerned, first and foremost, with knowing the kind of person an otherwise qualified teacher is.[2]

Consider the following characteristics as you observe classes and try to choose the best teacher for your child. You might not find one teacher with all these qualities, or your child's needs may require other qualities, but it's a good place to begin.

- Shows openness, warmth, and caring. The number one reason students give for dropping out of school is the feeling that no one cares about them.
- Encourages questions and gives kids opportunities to

dialogue. A recent study of California elementary teachers who had the most significant, positive influence on their students showed that they asked questions, used problem-solving techniques, and initiated discussion to raise students' level of comprehension.

- Encourages a child's interests, hobbies, or skills. Anita Price, a teacher who has taught preschool through middle school, says, "I feel I can really teach a child once I find out who he is and where his interests are. With every child, there is *something* that will open the door."
- Motivates students creatively. In addition to textbook and workbook assignments, the teacher assigns projects and enrichment activities.
- Administers balanced discipline. Discipline must be firm but caring, so the classroom is organized but not rigid.
- Models what is taught. As this poem says:

No written word or spoken plea
Can teach young hearts what they should be
Not all the books on all the shelves
But what the teachers are themselves.[3]

- Promotes parent involvement. The teacher includes parents in the classroom, communicates with them about their concerns, and updates them on their child's progress.
- Is knowledgeable and enthusiastic about subject matter.
- Has an ability to respond to and appreciate different personalities, ethnic backgrounds, and learning styles. The teacher has a willingness to teach the material so that children with different ways of processing information can learn.

- Praises students for both their efforts and their performances. Sincere encouragement and appreciation bring out the best in a child and foster a good teacher-student relationship.

The warm glow from a teacher's approval can last for a lifetime. "I'll never forget my second-grade teacher, Mrs. Woodward," a young mom told me. "That was 30 years ago. No matter what my score on a test or assignment, she found something positive to say. She smiled at me! I loved her and worked my hardest for her all year long."

CHILDREN CONNECTING WITH TEACHERS

Since any relationship is a two-way street, the child's attitude also affects his relationship with teachers. Several factors help children get along with their teachers. Pediatrician Dr. Robert Block says most teachers appreciate a child who shows a willingness to try. He tells parents to encourage their children to try by rewarding their efforts—not just their results. "If parents display disappointment over their child's lack of early success, their child may be afraid to take risks and try new tasks in the future. However, a child who applies himself to his work will make better connections with his teachers than a child who tries only once and gives up," Dr. Block told me.

Children who have close, loving relationships with parents form better connections with teachers, coaches, and other adults. Dr. Margie Golick, chief psychologist at the Learning Center at McGill-Montreal Children's Hospital, says, "A child will be receptive to a teacher's instruction only if he has learned to care about the adults in his world. This kind of caring grows out of his own experiences of being cared about, respected, and loved. If experience has taught him to like grownups, he might even be able to make allowances now and then for the unreasonable behavior of a crabby teacher."[4]

Verbally skilled children who enjoy open communication at home also bond better with teachers. Kids who know how to talk to the teacher, ask questions without being argumentative, express what they need, and ask for help can form relationships with their teachers more easily. Listening skills are also important and can be learned by conversing with parents and siblings around the dinner table or at other times during the day. Children need to learn not only how to listen, but also how to follow directions, to function in a group, and to be patient when the teacher can't give them immediate attention.

In addition, if you promote a love of learning and instill the value of education in your child, he will establish better relationships with his teachers. Parents need to support the teacher and school at home. "When education is not supported at home, it's more difficult for the student and teacher to bond," Dr. Block adds.

A parent's view of teachers affects their child's attitude, especially during his early years of education. If parents see teachers as allies, their children tend to have a positive attitude toward their teachers. It's important to talk positively about teachers in front of your children. If you disagree with the teacher about how he handled a situation, approach him directly rather than venting your negative feelings in front of your child. Negative impressions can last long after the problem is resolved.

FINDING A GOOD MATCH

Schools are becoming more and more receptive to parents' choosing their child's teachers (especially parents of young children). Because the early educational years set the stage for their entire education, children need to be fostered in a supportive learning environment, especially in the early elementary years through grade four. During these years, children are learning all the basics of reading, writing, computation, and thinking skills and need to focus on their studies. Personality clashes with teachers can be distracting to the learning process. Hopefully, children will discover early that school is a welcoming, exciting place to learn and grow.

Some argue that parents should not request a specific teacher and that any problem their child encounters with an instructor is just part of the schooling process. However, Dr. Burron says that a teacher's personality is far more important than the teacher's credentials, the physical environment of the school, the quality of the materials, or any other factors.[5] Whenever possible, request your child's teacher. Following are ways to select a teacher for your child.

- Make inquiries before moving into a new school district. Ask school officials if the district has a policy that allows parents to request a teacher, and if so, to whom the request should be made. At most schools, teachers meet during the last month in the spring to do class placements. Many factors are considered: for example, the ratio of boys to girls, personalities, which students can't be together, and the balance of ability levels. It's a complicated process.

  If your school district has a policy allowing parents to request a given teacher, talk to other parents and teachers, visit the school, and observe classrooms. Watch for teachers who would make a good match for your child. If you think a certain teacher would work best with your child, send your request in writing to the principal in the spring before class lists are created.

- In schools where there is no specific policy, it is usually possible to have your request for a specific teacher honored, especially if you have already built a good relationship with school personnel. Kris, a Texas mom, says, "I always pray that my children will get a teacher who meets their needs at that particular stage in their life. Along with that, I talk to the principal and let him know I have a vested interest in the *whole* school and am concerned for *all* the kids' needs. He knows I'm not just watching out for my kids.

  "Our third-grader has had a problem with recurrent stomachaches. We haven't discovered the cause yet, but I told the principal that a certain teacher would be best for my child considering his needs and strengths. Then I asked, 'What do you think?' I'm willing to listen and have an approach that is team-oriented and non-threatening on my part. We work together."
- If you've recently moved into a new area and don't know the school or the teachers, or if requests for specific teachers are not honored, consider following Teresa Caraway's example.

Each spring Teresa, the mother of two sons, makes an appointment with the school principal and expresses appreciation for the growth and learning her boys have experienced as a result of being at the school. She wants him to know she and her husband appreciate his leadership.

Teresa follows up with a thank you letter a few days later: "Thank you for meeting with me. Thanks, too, for the energy, time, and commitment you put forth to make our school the best. You've made a difference in our boys' life and education, and we are grateful. Have a great summer. I'm looking forward to working with you next year. See you in August! Sincerely, . . ."

When the principal returns to school after his summer break, Teresa calls him and schedules an appointment. She gives him a letter that says, "All the teachers are very good and qualified, but

Whether your school permits you to choose a teacher or not, your child's school experience will be more positive if you build a relationship with the teacher.

we know the bottom line is that different personalities complement each other and can make a difference in a child's learning. I need your assistance and leadership in providing a good match for our boys." She lists her boys' strengths and weaknesses for the principal. She also gives him the former teacher's recommendations for what type of teacher best motivates each of her boys to learn. (See sample letter below.)

Teresa doesn't specify which teachers she wants her boys to have but rather leaves the decision with the principal. "I trust his professionalism and have been pleased with the teacher he has selected for each boy."

Whether your school permits you to choose a teacher or not, your child's school experience will be more positive if you build a relationship with the teacher. In the next chapter we'll look at some ways to do that.

TERESA CARAWAY'S SAMPLE LETTER

August 5, 1991

Dr. Linda DeSpain, Principal
Harvest Hills Elementary
Oklahoma City, OK 73162

Dear Dr. DeSpain,

As a parent of two new students moving into the Harvest Hills attendance area, I enjoyed meeting you in May and touring the school. I have no doubts that this upcoming school year will be the beginning of an excellent academic experience for my children at Harvest Hills under your leadership.

I completed the boys' enrollment applications in May and appreciated the opportunity to provide some information regarding their individual characteristics. Since this will be their first year at Harvest Hills, I feel that their classroom placement is extremely important.

My oldest son, Taylor Caraway, will be entering the fourth grade. He can be shy but is generally confident and a self-starter. He needs a teacher who encourages creativity beyond the more traditional workbook learning to challenge and stretch him to his fullest potential. He is a bright student who enjoys exposure to new and challenging information. With a strong visual memory, if given one example of how to do a math problem or assignment, he will take off without a lot of explanation. He would benefit from a teacher who enjoys discovering an individual student's abilities and designing special projects that produce maximum growth during the academic year. Taylor is an inquisitive student and a motivated learner with good self-discipline skills.

My youngest son, Carson Caraway, will be entering the second grade this year. He is shy and extremely sensitive. He needs a teacher who is an encourager and a self-confidence builder. He needs a rah-rah cheerleader-type to say, "Do your best to stay on track," a teacher who will stretch and push him in a positive manner but is sensitive to student stress. With a strong auditory bent, Carson needs a teacher who explains and clarifies orally and walks him through the steps of a problem. He would benefit from a teacher who maintains structure in a calm, gentle, but down-to-business manner. Carson is a good student who needs to maintain a high level of success to maximize his capabilities. Carson is extremely well mannered and cooperative in the classroom.

I appreciate your time and concern regarding classroom placement for Taylor and Carson. I believe all faculty at Harvest Hills are excellent teachers; it is just that there are better match-ups between teachers and students that allow for maximum growth. I trust your professional leadership in this area and look forward to a great school year. I feel quite fortunate to have the opportunity to build a partnership with you and the staff at Harvest Hills in the education of Taylor and Carson. If you have any questions or if I can help in any way, please contact me. Thank you again.

Sincerely,
Teresa Caraway

CHAPTER 5

Building a Working Relationship with Teachers

Esther Portillo, a single parent in Simsbury, Connecticut, works 50 hours a week at two jobs. She has found that building friendship with the teacher is a key to getting her daughters the support and help they need to succeed at school. Because she can't volunteer in the classroom, she meets the girls' teachers at the start of the school year, she tries not to miss conferences, and she keeps in touch with the school.

Following the first conference, because the family's native language was Spanish, the teacher arranged tutoring in English for Esther's second-grader during the school day. Esther also took her to the library to play add-and-subtract games on the public computer once a week to help with math. After grades come out, Esther always asks the teacher what needs to be achieved in the next term and how she can help her daughters improve.

"The results are always positive," says Esther. "When the teacher knows I care and am concerned, she has suggestions of ways to help the girls."

When Emily started first grade at a new school, 50 percent of the class was already reading. Emily had been in a good developmental kindergarten but had no letter recognition or decoding skills. After Susan got to know the first-grade teacher, she began to help Emily catch up.

"The teacher really opened her heart and all of her information and resources to me, and we worked together," says Susan. "She suggested activities and I worked at home every day with Emily. By the end of the year she was reading at the top of her class."

The teacher's expectations for your child will be higher because she knows you care.

For most of us, time is short and our days are packed! But as Esther and Susan did, many parents are finding that contact with the teacher is a high priority. "I either have time to organize the spring carnival or be involved in activities that expose me to their teachers," says Carolyn Curtis, a Michigan mom. "I can't do it all. So I help the teacher once a week and I conference with them. I've found that having a good relationship with the teacher is *invaluable*."

BENEFITS OF BRIDGE-BUILDING

When you get to know your child's teacher:

- You build a bridge of communication, so that if a problem arises or you have a concern, you already have a foundation on which you and the teacher can work together in solving the problem.

- You earn the right to say something when you feel inappropriate things are being taught. "There are going to be places we disagree so we'd better build a relationship right away," says Jay Abramson, an Avon, Connecticut, dad. "That way when there's a problem, the teachers know we aren't attacking as foes, but we are there as friend to friend. They know we honor them as teachers, knowing they have many strong attributes, but we are still dealing with the problem.

  "The teachers aren't dealing with some anonymous crackpots who get upset about one textbook issue and then disappear," adds Jay. "We've laughed and shared and helped one another. We might say, 'We're coming from this perspective in creation science and would appreciate some sensitivity on this issue.' With that approach, we've never had a science teacher reject our point of view."
- The teacher's expectations for your child will be higher because she knows you care, that you have high expectations for your child's education, and that you're doing your part at home to support learning. The attitude of "We're in this together," and "I want the best for my child; how can I help?" builds accountability and support.
- You will know more about what goes on in the classroom, what needs to be mastered during the school year, and you can keep in touch with your child's progress. You will know how to help him apply at home what's being learned at school and spot and solve little problems before they become big ones.

THE SCHOOL'S APPROACH TO PARENTS

Parent involvement is boosted if a school is accessible, inviting, and attractive to parents, according to Dr. Dan Yunk, principal of Northview Elementary School of Manhattan, Kansas. Dr. Yunk, who speaks and visits schools all over the nation, finds that schools that say "Our parents don't care and don't support us" are usually schools that don't welcome parents as volunteers or encourage their input. This is an important characteristic to consider when you choose a school: Look for one with an open, welcoming attitude that encourages many different kinds of involvement by parents.

WHAT IF YOUR SCHOOL DOESN'T ENCOURAGE PARENT INVOLVEMENT?

If your efforts to get involved in your child's school are resisted, find out what the teacher's concerns are: Does she feel your presence interferes with your child's learning, or does she lack self-confidence? Does she see parents as a threat? Some teachers may feel that parents want to take over or that their desire to get involved indicates lack of confidence in the teacher's competency. Many teachers haven't had training in how best to involve parents.

Whatever you do, don't take "no" for an answer when you are trying to become involved at school. When parents are partners in education, schools and classrooms work better, and all children learn more.

Sometimes you can work individually with a teacher, or you may need to work with your principal or parent groups to find ways to become involved. In schools that have had little parent involvement in the past, a more structured and organized approach may be needed. You may need to go to school board meetings, get on the open agenda, and work to change board policy to *support* meaningful parental involvement and to make a place for parents to be involved with decision making, problem solving, and volunteering at school. Parents may have to reach out and take the first step.[1]

THE IMPORTANCE OF PARENTS' POSITIVE ATTITUDES

Our attitude is also an important part of bridge-building with school personnel. As parents, we can recognize that the reason most people teach is that they genuinely care about kids. Of course, we may encounter people who should have chosen a different career path or are difficult personalities, but let's not judge the whole profession by these few.

It's important to listen to what the teacher has to say. Beth, a Colorado mom, was told by her son's fourth-grade teacher that she needed to back off and let him speak for himself. She didn't like hearing it, but it was true; she needed to let her son take more initiative. As she did, his ability to relate to his teachers verbally increased. He grew in confidence and learned to speak up instead of depending on Mom to make things right at school. If Beth had ignored the teacher's suggestion, her son would have missed a valuable opportunity for growth.

"Give teachers a chance," says Susan Gainer, a mom in Edmond, Oklahoma. "I always try to mentally give the teacher the benefit of the doubt when my child is concerned. From the outset, I view the teacher in the light that she is trying to do the best for my child. I have failed my child often, even with the best intentions, so I must, at least, offer a teacher who may deal with 200 individuals that same latitude. I go with the attitude of 'What can I do to help you?' "

"I expect teachers to respect me for my role in my child's life, just as I respect their professional ability," says Kris Olson, a Waco, Texas, mom. "I know what is best for my child in a lot of ways, but the teacher is trained to teach and can be objective about my child, so I can gain valuable insights about strengths and weaknesses and things we need to be working on. I let the teacher know I'm available to help my child, that I know my child is not perfect, and I can work with her to do what is appropriate to solve a problem."

When the teacher feels valued as a professional and appreciated, a rapport and working relationship develops that greatly benefits your child's education and increases the possibility that his needs will be met at school.

How can we build that relationship when we can't be in the classroom every week, either because we need to be at home with younger children or have a job outside the home? Let's look at some ways through the initial meeting or conference at the beginning of the year, continuing communication through notes, a potpourri of simple ideas to show appreciation, and getting the most out of conferences.

MEETING THE TEACHER

The beginning of the school year is the ideal time to meet the teacher. Going by the classroom during "teacher's work and in-service days" or stopping by before or after school (when you're picking up your child) the first week lets the teacher know you are available and interested in your child's education. It's best to make an appointment because in-service days are full of meetings. If you take the initiative and keep it short, the teacher gets the message: Here is a parent who is responsible, here is a parent I can call if a problem develops, and here is a family that will support the child's learning.

One mom who stops by during the week before school says she takes her child along (this is especially helpful with a kindergartner or first-grader or if you are going to a new school) so she can be familiar with the room. She and the teacher spend only 15 to 20 minutes chatting, but the teacher tells them what they'll be doing during the year, what they can expect the first day, etc. With the chance to interact with the teacher, her son feels confident on the first day of school, and mom and teacher have made the first step toward building rapport.

Even if you only have time to stop by and say hello, introduce yourself, and perhaps bring a flower from your garden to brighten the teacher's desk, you will have made a positive first contact.

AN EARLY CONFERENCE

Many parents find an individual parent-teacher conference sometime during the first three weeks of school helps greatly to build a working relationship.

"Even though you're busy, and time is tight, it's important to sit down with the teacher and talk one-to-one," says Teresa Caraway, a working mom. "I do this the second or third week of school, depending on how things are going." An in-person conference is best, but if time doesn't permit, a phone conference can establish communication.

"Any conference in the first to third week of school is positive, and at that time I let the teacher know in a gracious way that I feel it's our primary responsibility to educate my child, and that she is my support and I'm grateful for her," says Carolyn Curtis. "I think this takes a tremendous load off the teacher. I've always found teachers positive about my approach, in fact, grateful that they weren't going to have to assume the role of parent because it was adequately assumed by me. That allows them to fulfill the role of teacher! It helps them know what kind of working relationship I expect, and that I will be supportive during the year."

What could you discuss during this early conference?

- You could ask the teacher what she's noticed so far concerning strengths and weaknesses of your child. (This tells you how perceptive the teacher is about your child, and if she isn't aware of some things, you can provide information.)
- You could share what your child has enjoyed about school and what seems to be a struggle for him or what he needs help with.
- You could ask what short- and long-range projects and units are coming up for the class, and what the homework policy, expectations for class behavior, and teacher's goals are for the year.
- You could ask what you can do at home to support your child's learning.

Then following the report card period, request a few minutes of the teacher's time to conference concerning your child's progress and any recent standardized test scores. Schools typically require only two conferences between parent and teacher each year and some, only one, which is not enough.

"It's worth 30 minutes of my time to have that interaction with the teacher," said one mom, "even if it's a telephone conference." It holds the teacher accountable to verbalize your child's special strengths and weaknesses, how he is progressing in weak areas, and what you can do to help at home. It also heads off problems before they get serious.

Begin the conference by sharing something positive the teacher is doing that you appreciate or how she has helped your child in the classroom. The day before, talk to your child about how school is going and any subject he might be struggling in. Bring a list of questions you want to discuss, such as:

- How does my child get along with classmates?
- What grade level is my child reading at, and what grade level is he functioning at in math?
- What are my child's best and worst subjects?
- How is his behavior in class? Does he pay attention? Does he use time wisely and turn in classwork and homework consistently?
- Does my child need special help in any academic subject?
- What are his scores on achievement or intelligence tests he has taken in the past year?

An attitude of "How can I help?" aids in building a partnership between parent and teacher. Following up with notes is important after the initial contact and after conferences.

COMMUNICATING THROUGH NOTES

When you're a busy parent who can't be in the classroom, notes are an effective way to keep up communication with a teacher. Notes don't replace regular in-person conferences, but they serve two purposes:

- They let your child know you're in touch with the teacher.
- They let the teacher know you're involved, appreciate his or her efforts, and that you care.

You don't have to be on the school premises to keep in touch with teachers! Writing a note takes only a few moments but can have a *big impact*. One veteran teacher told me she kept a thank you note from a parent in her desk drawer all year and brought it out and reread it on her hardest days! Many teachers feel unappreciated and go the whole year without a single note that lets them know what they're doing right.

Here's what one mom's experience was in sending a note to her daughter's teachers:

"This year, at your suggestion, I sent notes to Heather's and Lauren's teachers, thanking them for specific things. (I had not mentioned the problems Heather had in first grade, but the net effect is that she has lower than usual self-esteem.) In the note to Heather's teacher, I thanked her for the individual attention Heather had received in her care and how this had a positive effect on her self-esteem. In Lauren's teacher's note, I thanked her for making learning to read fun. I described the light that would beam in Lauren's eyes when she began recognizing the words she was reading.

"It just so happened that the teachers received these notes the morning of Meet the Teacher night. Since I wouldn't be able to attend for the whole evening, I arrived at the school 30 minutes before it was to begin. I introduced myself to both teachers and left a tape recorder in Lauren's class to get all the information. My husband, Ken, sat through the session in Heather's class.

"That night when I got home, Ken went over his notes from Mrs. Brown's class. Then he told me that Mrs. Brown pointed out to him that Heather needed better self-esteem! She indicated that she was going to work on it, too. Later, I listened to the tape from Lauren's teacher and heard her describe how exciting it is to 'see the light that beams in a child's eyes when they begin recognizing the words they're reading.'

"I don't think that was a coincidence. Lauren's teacher, although polite before, has been measurably warmer toward me since the note. I think the notes helped establish a positive relationship with the teachers and planted the seed for what my children needed in a very positive light."

You can include a note to go back with the "Friday Folder" if one is sent home each week with all the work your child has done, or send a note any school day with your child.

Here are some ideas that you can include in notes to teachers:

> "Thank you for the extra help you gave Jay on his word problems and for the multiplication table practice sheets you sent home. We think he's slowly gaining confidence and appreciate all you're doing to encourage him."

> "Cary doesn't understand parts of the diagramming process. Could you explain to her again how you want it done? Many thanks."

> "I notice you take the time to write notes and comments in the corners of many graded papers. I admire this, since you probably have graded 10 quadrillion papers since you started teaching. It is the effort you put into correcting these papers and your teaching that reflects to me the depth of your dedication to excellence."

> "We are concerned about Jennifer's big drop on her history test. What can be done at school and at home to help get her back on the right track?"

> "The Read-a-Thon you had for the third-graders was a big hit! Michael is reading (and enjoying it) more than he ever has. We're thankful for your creative ideas that motivate him."

A follow-up note after Open House is a great way to build rapport:

> "Your classroom was decorated in such a bright and happy way. I'm glad Sarah can come to your room each day. We appreciate the handouts you gave us at Open House last night on grading standards, books used, and projects coming up. We look forward to a fine year at Roosevelt School."

And don't forget the support people who probably don't get a lot of feedback or appreciation, such as the cafeteria workers, bus drivers, librarians, and music and art teachers. They work together as a team to make the school environment a good one for your child to learn and grow in. You can encourage the support staff and keep them aware of your child's needs and what you appreciate with a note, such as this one to the librarian:

> "Thanks for making Carrie's first media experience positive and helping her find a book she was interested in. She was excited to share the book with us at the dinner table. You helped make her first week at this new school a great start."

A POTPOURRI OF IDEAS TO SHOW APPRECIATION

It's the small kindnesses that are such a blessing and build rapport and a groundwork for working together. Most of us are so busy we never get around to doing the big spectacular things, but little thoughtful deeds can communicate a lot of appreciation. Here are some ideas that don't take a lot of time:

- When you (or your child) bake a batch of cookies, brownies, muffins, or treats for the weekend, wrap two or three in plastic wrap, put a ribbon around it, and attach a note: "Have a good day. From the Johnsons." Send it with your child to school.

- At Christmas baking time, suggest to each mom you know that she bake an extra dozen cookies. Several moms can take them to the teachers' lounge, put a red tablecloth on the table, spread out their holiday cookies, and brighten the day of all the teachers.
- Write a Christmas card to each of your child's teachers (especially good in middle school or high school because it would be expensive to provide a gift for each one!) expressing appreciation. "Every Christmas I write each of my girls' high school teachers a card saying that Christmas is a time of giving and that I appreciate the gift of their time and energy, the gift they are giving to my daughter of a good education," says Carolyn Curtis. "If nothing else, it gives them a moment to pause and know they're appreciated and a reason to evaluate their teaching and live up to a higher expectation."
- Send an apple, orange, or other fresh fruit any time of the year.
- Pick zinnias, daisies, mums, or other flowers out of your garden, wrap in a damp paper towel and plastic wrap to keep fresh, and send them with your child or deliver personally.
- Send a bookmark or colorful inspirational poster that relates to education for display in the classroom.
- Let your child make an "ABC Book for My Teacher" to show appreciation on Valentine's Day or a holiday, with each page containing a different letter:

A is for the apple that sits on her desk.
B is for the books Mrs. Jones reads to us each day.
C is for crayons we all love to draw with.
D is for your determination in working with us;
and so on through the alphabet. Have your child illustrate each page, staple the pages together and make a cover.

- Look for a need in the classroom that you can fill. One mom bought a box of tissues and some special stickers.
- Recycle your good magazines. Instead of throwing them away, tie a bow around a stack of them and give to the class as resources for reports, extra reading, clipping pictures for craft projects, etc. (Check first with the teacher to see if the class already receives the magazine.)
- Make a coupon for one hour of volunteer time for cutting out bulletin board letters at home, being an extra hand in the classroom on a hectic day, or whenever the teacher most needs it. You or your child can decorate the coupon, put it in an envelope, and give it as "A Gift of Time."
- Give encouragement—through a kind word, a special smile—when you see the principal, teachers, office workers, custodian, or even the bus driver. "Develop a relationship with the people who your child is spending his day with," suggests one mom. "Encourage them by showing God's love through your actions and words. There is such heaviness in the world; people hunger for kindness!"
- Deliver or have delivered a small pizza, something nice to drink, and maybe a little nosegay of flowers to your child's teacher during "Teacher Appreciation Week" or the

teacher's birthday and take her out to lunch right in her own classroom.

- Provide an Open House meal. This takes more time so it's not for everyone, but it can pay huge dividends in terms of building relationships. Because the first week of school is so hectic with beginning activities and Open House, one mom prepared a very simple meal for her children's second- and third-grade teachers. She just tripled the recipe for what her family was having that night and brought it to school in a box with a small vase of flowers from her garden. The meal contained stew, cornbread, a stick of butter, and a bowl of pudding and cream.

  "I have four small children, so it had to be simple!" Linda said. "I brought it in after school for them to take home and enjoy with their families before Open House. The teachers were so blessed that they shared the story with the other teachers. Later that week, I was stopped and thanked by the principal. God's love surely shined through a small willing vessel!"
- Provide Open House hospitality. When teachers live out of the district or have so much to do that they don't go home before Open House or other evening activities at school, you could provide a boxed dinner for the teacher to eat at her desk.
- Invite the teacher to your child's birthday party. Send an invitation that says, "We know you are busy and may not be able to stay, but we'd love for you to come by after school for cake and ice cream."
- Remember to say "thank you." We all love being appreciated. Besides the benefit to the teacher hearing you

express your appreciation, it is an important lesson to teach your child. By modeling appreciation, you are helping your child see you give honor to the teacher and affirm her efforts. This can have a wonderful effect on your child's attitude and lay the groundwork for his thoughtfulness to others as he grows up.

MIDDLE SCHOOL AND HIGH SCHOOL: KEEPING IN TOUCH

Parent-teacher conferences in middle and high school are often not scheduled or encouraged by the school. Even in schools that encourage parent involvement at the elementary level, the ball is dropped and less is done to invite parent partnership from middle school on. At the very time parents need information and guidance on how to be involved, they get less information from school personnel.

As a result, many middle and high school parents get out of touch with what goes on at school. A nationwide survey of almost 25,000 eighth-graders showed that half of them never even discussed school with their parents and only half of the parents had any contact with the school.

It's true that contact is harder at this stage. Your child may have six or seven teachers, rather than one in a self-contained classroom. His school-day schedule is more complicated, and the middle school itself may be three or four times larger than the elementary school. *But staying in touch is just as vital as in the early years!*

Jay Abramson and his wife, Liz, have found there are no parent-teacher conferences scheduled at the middle and high schools their boys attend. "Even though the school doesn't initiate it, we call and set up a time to meet each son's teachers as a group," says

Jay. "Some of the teachers have asked, 'Why do you want to meet with us? Your boys are doing fine.'

"We tell them, 'Because we see their education as our responsibility, we want to talk to you about how it's going. We want to know if there's anything we can do to support what you're doing in the classroom.'"

In every single meeting, Liz and Jay have gained insight they needed and been able to tackle little problems before they became big. For example, their 12-year-old son, Jesse, had stopped bringing homework home, and his grades were sliding. The Abramsons discussed Jesse's problem with his teachers and discovered that they, too, were frustrated because they knew he was capable of more. However, they would have waited until his grades fell to a D before calling a conference. Together they decided that in the future Jesse would come to the desk and look at each teacher's assignment book, make sure he had written down that night's homework correctly, and have his teacher initial his assignment sheet at the end of the class period. Each night, after completing the homework assignments, he would show them to his parents.

"Jesse wasn't thrilled about this arrangement, but it helped him establish a good pattern," Jay said. "After a month, he was back on track with his grades up." Students in middle school and high school need their parents' guidance and involvement, especially in helping select appropriate courses they need to take. Many students find themselves in a mishmash of courses. In a nationwide study, of all the eighth-graders who intended to go to college, less than one-third were taking the college preparatory courses they needed for admission.

If you're a middle or high schooler's parent, keep in touch by:

- Being familiar with the student/parent handbook and reading all the information that comes home from school.
- Meeting your child's teachers early (even if there are five or six) and letting them know you want to be contacted about any problem.
- Networking with other parents of teens. Get to know them so you can compare notes on curfews, activities, and common problems. This parent-to-parent contact is very important leading up to and during the adolescent years!
- Being a part of planning your child's course selection for junior high and high school.
- Attending as many school events as you can. If your teen has a drama, athletic, or musical event, be there. He may not say "Thanks for coming," but he always looks for you!

CHAPTER 6

Knowing What Your Child Is Being Taught

When Donna Thurman's nine-year-old son, Zach, asked for a pillow to take to school, she asked what it was for. "I don't know," he answered. "I think we're laying down." The next day Donna did not send a pillow; instead she spoke to the resource teacher in charge of the activity. When she asked about the pillow, the teacher told her that the students were going to lie on the floor and learn relaxation techniques as part of a session on self-esteem and coping with stress.

Feeling that the activity was inappropriate, Donna politely objected to it and asked the school administrators to get parental approval for all supplemental activities.

Because of this and other parents' appeals, the school now

notifies parents about any special programs and gains their approval before implementing them in the classroom.

STAYING IN TOUCH

One of the keys to keeping in touch with what is being taught in school is to *listen* to your children. Let your child know he can talk with you about his classes whenever he has a question or feels uncomfortable about what he is learning. "If children are brushed off and Mom and Dad have no time for their questions, concerns, and problems about school, they clam up and don't share," says Fern Nichols, founder of Moms in Touch, International. Parents need to be there to reinforce truth, to discuss issues, and to take children to the Word when there are questions about what they are studying.

"Even if I'm in my home office during their homework time, they know we can sit down and talk about things, and that they are my number one priority," says Fern.

DIALOGUE AND DISCUSSION IN THE FAMILY

"It scares us when our kids hear opinions and views contrary to our own; we want to plug up their ears," says Jay Abramson. "Instead, we need to help them understand what we believe. We can tell them, 'You're going to hear other views. We want you to become a discoverer and to learn to think inductively and deductively, rather than parrot what we've told you. We form our own ideas and learn to think by looking at a topic from every side. Scripture tells us to examine truth.'

"We talk, talk, talk at the dinner table," says Jay, "and right now we're dealing with evolution. Each student in our 15-year-old son's class was asked to bring something that represented their view of how the universe began. So we started talking about what he would bring. We discussed it together off and on for several days and got him books and tapes on the topic.

"We didn't say, 'Here's what you must present,' but talked about what he thinks and what is the truth." Jay's son decided to share with his class books and diagrams documenting the creation.

The von Kleist family has found that dialogue with their children is a vital part of supporting them in school. "At dinnertime, we like to review what went on at school," says Rick von Kleist. "I ask, 'What did you do today? How do you feel about what happened?' " His wife is a kindergarten and first-grade teacher, so their dinner conversation often centers around what went on at school. "My daughter knows I'm really concerned about her school experience; I want to make sure it's positive. I want to know what she's learning. At bedtime I always read a Bible story and sometimes we read and discuss a story like *Lady and the Tramp*."

Justin Shepherd, 14, attends ninth grade in the local high school in Fairfax County, Virginia. There he encounters values different from his own and his family's. However, he is intellectually and spiritually prepared to defend his faith. Each day as his father drives him to school, they talk about what he will be studying in class.

Discussion time is endangered for most families because of our incredibly fast-paced lives. It's difficult to find the time to talk. For example, as I am writing this chapter, I am looking at our family's schedule for tonight. Alison has a high school swim meet, Chris has basketball practice, and Holmes, a meeting at church. Meetings and activities strip away time to talk. We may have to find other times to have those discussions, at the dinner table, on the way to soccer practice or to school, over a snack before bedtime, or even late at night!

Ellen Shepherd, mother of eight and vice president of the Church and Family Resource Council in Fairfax County, Virginia, tells parents, "No matter what car problems, job problems, or time pressures you're facing, there's a lot going on in your child's life at school that needs your support and attention."

Studies show that family discussion is vital to a young person's success in school. One study showed the correlation between a student's home situation and his school performance. It wasn't necessarily his IQ or financial situation, but rather the amount of time *he talked with his parents about what he was learning in school* that was the deciding factor. According to the study, the most conversation-provoking questions were not "How did you do in school?" or "What grades did you make today?" but "What did you talk about in science? Do you agree with that? What are you learning in history? What do you think about it? Have you changed your opinion?"

KNOWING TEXTBOOKS AND CLASSROOM CONTENT

Parents who read their children's textbooks gain a lot of knowledge about what they're learning. "I'm involved in my sons' homework, so we often read passages from their textbooks together," says Judy Hartsock, a Norman, Oklahoma, mom. "I read the geography textbook, and when the class studied world religions, such as Buddhism and Islam, we talked about 'Is this right? What do you think?' I want my children to be able to discern the facts and make wise choices."

Judy also prays about the subjects her children choose for book reports. She encourages her sons to select books by outstanding Christian leaders and role models, such as Orel Hershiser's *Out of the Blue*, Dave Dravecky's *Comeback*, or Corrie Ten Boom's *The Hiding Place*. Giving these book reports orally is also a great inspiration to their classmates.

"I read through each textbook our children had," says Susan Gainer of Edmond, Oklahoma. "We are privileged to live in a state where lawmakers passed a law giving parents the right to refuse course material counter to their religious beliefs. Some of the textbooks are wholesome and high quality, but I have exercised this option by refusing some reading material and substituting more appropriate books. I also kept my daughter out of science class when certain sex- and drug-education materials were substituted for science material."

When your older children bring their books home for book covers at the beginning of school is a good time to sit down and scan through them, getting an overview of the content, philosophy, and chapter headings and discussing with your kids what's ahead in the course. Then read textbooks regularly with your kids and monitor their homework so you know what they're learning.

What should you look for in a textbook? Often it's what has been omitted that's of most importance. Many times, history books don't adequately cover the importance of Christianity in America or around the world; biology books may not even mention creationism; and health books may downplay the role of motherhood and homemaking. These omissions provide wonderful opportunities for you to teach your child. You can "fill in the gaps" left by the texts.[1]

Consider the weight a book assigns to a certain issue. Does it seem lopsided in its presentation of a subject? Does the author have an agenda? If so, what is it? A textbook writer's influence should not be underestimated. A historian's treatment of a historical event or person can significantly impact your child's view of history. For example, you could balance the average textbook's approach to the discovery of America (that Columbus discovered it by accident while seeking a trade route to the Indies) by reading to your children from Peter Marshall's book *The Light and the Glory*.[2] This book is told from the point of view that God had a plan for this country, and He intervened repeatedly to ensure its coming to pass.

GETTING YOUR OWN COPY OF THE TEXTBOOK

First, ask your child's teacher to let you borrow the book. If the teacher doesn't have an extra copy, he may be able to borrow one from another teacher or find an old copy in the storeroom. If you still come up empty, go to the curriculum/textbook coordinator at the district level and ask if a copy is available from any school or storage warehouse. Finally, if you are really dedicated to getting the book, write to the publisher and buy it. It's a small investment to make for your child's education.[3]

Obtain a copy of the curriculum, a plan of the objectives for that grade, and the methods and resources that will be used to teach it from the teacher (especially if the school has site-based management) or school district office. If the curriculum is controversial, school personnel may be resistant to share the material with you. New curriculum is usually available for review by parents several weeks *before* adoption by the school or district. Stay in touch to know when new curriculum is introduced and take advantage of the opportunity to review it. If volunteers are recruited to serve on textbook and/or curriculum committees, be sure to sign up!

Eric Buehrer, president of Gateways to Better Education, advises caution when reviewing material: "If you think you have found something of real concern in the curriculum, show it to several other people to get their perspective. It is easy to find 'questionable' things if you go looking for them. Parents have sent me copies of curricula in which they highlighted every occurrence of words like *visualize*, *image*, and *global*. Apparently, even the mere mention of these words were red flags to these parents that the program was obviously New Age."[4] Avoid overreacting. Look at the content and the program's overall objectives. Consider the program's underlying philosophy, which is often stated in the introduction.

Use the curriculum to interact with your child. Ask him what he thinks of the class or if he enjoys it. Find out if he has any questions, or if he is looking forward to studying a certain subject.

WHEN YOU HAVE A CONCERN ABOUT A TEXTBOOK OR CURRICULUM

Debbie Marsh, a Washington mother of three, became concerned one October when her fourth-grade daughter, Kendall, began having nightmares. After talking with her, Debbie realized the nightmares were related to the in-class reading of a story in their new literature textbook from the *Impressions Language Arts Curriculum*. They read the book together and Kendall pointed out the stories that frightened her. Debbie read the stories and found very graphic material. She read both of the books in the fourth-grade series and then categorized all the stories according to their content. For example, she labeled stories having positive or negative values, frightening imagery, gang- or drug-related material, violence, suicide references, etc.

Debbie and her husband shared her evaluations with the child's teacher. "We're concerned about the quality of this material and we'd like our daughter to read something else," the Marshes said.

The teacher referred them to the principal. So Debbie graciously presented her text evaluation to the principal. He suggested she pick a story for them to read and discuss together. As they read the text aloud, Debbie pointed out her concerns, and the principal shared *his* interpretations of the story. He ended their appointment by saying he would discuss Debbie's request with his supervisor.

The next week the school informed Debbie that Kendall could follow an individual reading program. The teacher told Debbie that during the time the class read the assigned stories, Kendall could bring her Bible and read in the library. A few other students began to bring their Bibles, too, and to ask Kendall questions. Because of Debbie's gentle, yet well-prepared, analysis of the series, Kendall's fifth-grade teacher this year has chosen not to use the *Impressions* reading program.

Another parent, Roxanne Pierce of Oakland, Maine, also had problems with the *Impressions* material. "At the beginning of the year, I always ask to look at the reading book and other textbooks that will be used as part of the curriculum for the school year. Last year, the *Impressions* reading program was my only real conflict, along with school Halloween celebrations." Roxanne asked her daughter's teachers to exempt her from certain reading assignments. Her complaint led to a careful review and elimination of some of the stories.

Even though the Shepherds' son had always been a good math student, he was receiving a D in geometry. His parents made an appointment with the teacher to find out what the problem was. They learned that all his math homework and classwork had been completed on time and averaged a B. However, the teacher said he hadn't been turning in his "journal," and that had been the reason for his lowered math grade.

His parents discovered that the journal had nothing to do with geometry but included entries on the students' feelings, their home life, and other personal questions. When they objected to the journal as a violation of their son's privacy and asserted their parental rights in a respectful way, their son no longer had to do the journal and his grade went back up to a B.

Following are guidelines these and other parents have used to alert school personnel about their concerns:

- Be relationally pro-active. Before any problem arose, Debbie and Roxanne had already established a good working relationship with their children's teachers and principals. They knew the principal personally from having served at the school in a variety of volunteer capacities. Debbie was the homeroom mother and helped in the classroom once a week. She even designed and recruited other volunteers for a special read-aloud program designed to help children reading below their grade level. Debbie was able to share her concerns without alienating the teacher or principal because she didn't appear at the school only to complain.

  Paul Heath, a bookstore manager, father, and president of a parents' organization in a Minnesota school, suggests that going to school after a problem arises is like buying the fire engine after the fire. "Be ready before the fire starts—don't wait until it's raging! Develop a relationship with the teachers and administrators before a problem ignites."
- Be selective and follow channels. Exercise self-control in choosing when to voice your complaints. "If you complain

too often, you won't be heard when you have a serious problem or issue," said Wendy Flint. Ask yourself: What's going to be effective in the long-term interest of my child? How can I do what I feel I must do and still keep bridges between me and the school? Some things you can handle and discuss at home with your children; other concerns need to be expressed to school personnel. Pray for the wisdom to know the difference.

- Implement diplomacy. When you are dissatisfied with a textbook or a school policy, address a teacher first rather than a principal or administrator. "Many times quiet diplomacy is more successful than a vocal outcry at a public meeting," says Michael Ebert in "Liberals Malign Parents as 'Censors.' "[5]

  Speak with the classroom teacher or staff member who is directly involved with the problem. Express your concerns and listen to their response. Parents have the right to appeal decisions not in their child's interest.[6]

  If the meeting with the teacher is ineffective, address the principal or superintendent or even a school board member. If you continue to face opposition, go to the state level.

- Know your rights. Become familiar with state education laws and school board policies concerning a particular issue. Be aware of your rights as a parent of a public school student. You have the right to request that your child be excused from school activities, studying subjects, or reading books you object to on religious, moral, or other reasonable grounds. You also have the right to review your child's school records and look at official school policies.

Specifically, under the Protection of Pupil Rights Amendment (the Hatch Amendment) to the General Education Provisions Act, parents can take steps to prevent schools from undermining their children's beliefs and moral values. By writing to school officials, parents can request that they have the opportunity to give written consent (preferably after reviewing the material) before their children are exposed to anything that does not uphold their values or moral standards—curricula, textbooks, audiovisual materials, guest speakers, or supplementary assignments.

Examples of topics include: values clarification; death education (including abortion, euthanasia, and suicide); alcohol and drugs; sex education and related matters; guided fantasy and hypnotic techniques; and witchcraft, occultism, the supernatural, and Eastern mysticism.

For more information on "Religious Expression in Public Schools," see Appendix F. Order the booklet *Knowing Your Rights*, by Jay Sekulow, from the American Center for Law and Justice ([757] 226-2489; www.aclj.org).

- Request a meeting to discuss your concerns or complaints. Have your spouse, a friend, or another parent accompany you. Present an alternative solution to solve the problem. Be sure to follow up after the meeting.
- Pray about the process. Debbie and her husband asked God for wisdom for themselves, the teacher, and the principal. They sought God's guidance in approaching school personnel and asked the local Moms in Touch group to pray about the situation.
- Be gracious to the school faculty and administrators, says Fern Nichols. Graciousness is characterized by kindness,

courtesy, tactfulness, mercy, and compassion. Avoid approaching school personnel with an attitude of superiority. A calm, kind approach builds relationships, while a critical, harsh manner builds walls. Keep showing appreciation for the teachers' efforts and find a way to contribute your time or talent to make a better classroom and school.

Here are two more important ways to deal with textbook and curriculum issues: Equip your children and yourself, and have input in choosing textbooks before they get into the classroom.

EQUIPPING OUR CHILDREN

Carolyn Curtis, a Michigan mother of three, believes that *preparing and equipping* her children to deal with the content they will encounter in the classroom has helped them stand firm in their values. When a note was sent home informing parents of the sex education program for third to 12th grades, she evaluated and approved the programs.

"The main reason I got the family life education curriculum is to know how I need to prepare my child during the summer for the upcoming year," says Carolyn. She uses it as a guideline for her children's summer "homework" program.

Part of *their* "family life education curriculum" involved listening to the "Preparing for Adolescence" tape series by Dr. James Dobson. They then discussed the topics together. Carolyn answers her children's questions honestly and prepares them for what they will be learning at school.[7]

The summer her daughters turned 13, they each read *Sex: Desiring the Best*. The next summer they read Part 2 of the *Why Wait?* series entitled *Dating: Picking (and Being) a Winner*. The following summer, at age 15, each read *Love: Making It Last*.[8]

"They had already covered the material in discussion with us, but through the reading and workbook approach of the Josh McDowell series, they were able to internalize the concepts and values and make them their own," says Carolyn. This 'family curriculum' prepared them for the seventh-grade sex education courses. They were then able to filter what they were being taught through a biblical perspective.

"By the time we had finished our summer program, we felt like the girls were equipped to handle the material mentally, spiritually, and emotionally," said Carolyn. Their daughters felt confident volunteering information and sharing their Christian viewpoints in the classroom.

Lael Arrington's book *World-Proofing Your Kids* is an excellent resource for parents in helping to shape a child's worldview. In addition, the video series *Understanding the Times* by Summit Ministries provides an ideal preparation for any young person with which to face the anti-Christian philosophies in high schools, colleges, and the media.[9] The textbook and 60 video segments help open young people's eyes to the competing philosophies in the world and equip them with a solid Christian perspective on current views.

Preparing ourselves as parents is an important step to giving our children a biblical worldview.

The video series can also be used by individual families and youth groups. John Stack at Hazelwood Baptist Church in Hazelwood, Missouri, uses the *Understanding the Times* video as a Sunday evening series with his youth group, all of whom attend public schools. John hopes to equip the young people to be

Christian leaders. "When kids leave youth groups, they often go to secular colleges and get confused because they haven't seen Christianity work in the real world," he says. "This series helps them see the big picture, discover how to apply Scripture to what they are going to encounter in the secular world, and learn how to make an impact."

The *Understanding the Times* video series is also helpful for parents' groups or adult Sunday school classes to study. It can equip parents to challenge and train their young people to realize their God-given potential and deal with opposing worldviews.

Summit Ministries also offers eight or more two-week camp sessions in Manitou Springs, Colorado, each summer to teach young people about the three major worldviews (Christian, secular humanist, and Marxist-Leninist). Speakers come from around the country.

Preparing ourselves as parents is an important step to giving our children a biblical worldview. Many public school textbooks and materials are philosophically opposed to the Christian worldview. Three books can help parents cope with the ideological challenges presented by public schools: Francis Schaeffer's *The Christian Manifesto*, James Dobson's *Children at Risk*, and David A. Noebel's *Understanding the Times*. In addition, parents should have a working knowledge of issues such as creation vs. evolution, apologetics, biblical sex education, America's Christian heritage, etc.[10]

DEALING WITH SCHOOL-TO-WORK ISSUES

In the Introduction, I mentioned a relatively new trend called school-to-work, which is a federally-funded and designed program to prepare students for the workplace and institute career-awareness programs and job preparation in the curriculum of public schools.

Actually, though the movement seems novel, the concept isn't entirely new. Cooperative learning (where noncollege-bound students held part-time jobs as a component of vocational education in high school) dates back to the early 1900s. "Tech prep" programs that combine the last two years of high school with two years in a community college, leading to a technical degree, have been available, and internships and job shadowing have also been used to identify career options and help students make a smooth transition to college and career.

While there are some positive aspects of school-to-work, there are also real concerns, such as less time for core academics and college preparatory education, the high school diploma perhaps being replaced by a Certificate of Mastery, and the fear that students may be coerced too early into career paths. With that in mind, Eric Buehrer of Gateways to Better Education recommends questions and suggestions to use if your school district is integrating school-to-work in the curriculum:[11]

1. Contact elected officials, from Congress to school boards, and voice your concerns. Organize like-minded citizens to exert pressure for change. Write letters. Make phone calls and personal visits.
2. Ask for the teacher's course of study (such as fourth-grade science, sixth-grade math, Algebra II). It should outline three things: the course objectives, the standards of learning, and the method of assessment. It should be clear and specific, avoiding vague, nonmeasurable objectives. A well-written course of study should not exceed 10 pages.
3. Use the teacher's course of study to gently and politely hold the teacher accountable for following it. It's not uncommon for teachers to ignore it.

4. Be sure your child is exposed to career options beyond what the school promotes.
5. Be careful about the personal information gathered on your child. Ask to see your child's complete file, including computer records, at the end of the year.
6. Ask school officials why a student who is building a solid academic foundation for college should have to select a career path by grade 11 (or even earlier).
7. Ask who will decide whether a student has exhibited the behavioral qualities necessary for a Certificate of Initial Mastery.
8. Ask school officials who is liable for student safety at the work-site apprenticeship. In at least one case when a parent asked this question, the business owner and the school district both claimed the other party had the responsibility.

   (Contact Gateways to Better Education at 714-586-KIDS for more information on school-to-work and other public-school controversies and issues.)

VOLUNTEERING TO SERVE ON TEXTBOOK AND CURRICULUM REVIEW COMMITTEES

It's important to have input *before* the curriculum material enters the classroom. You can even suggest textbooks and help ensure that books and curriculum be of high quality. For example, *Of Pandas and People* presents arguments for both evolution and creation.[12] Parents are introducing the book for consideration for high school biology classes across the country.

"The school district doesn't operate in a vacuum," says Paul Heath. "It's supported by our taxes, but most people keep it at arms' length and don't have a hands-on mentality with the public schools."

Encourage your school board to adopt a three-pronged test for choosing curriculum: First, does it serve a legitimate academic purpose? Second, does it represent the noblest and most wholesome literature for young people? Third, do all parents involved find it acceptable?

Paul Heath was asked to do double duty by serving on the Book Review Committee in addition to his job as PTO president because the principal couldn't find enough interested parents. "It's not time intensive," says Paul. "The committee meets once or twice a month in the evening. But this group can have a tremendous influence on the books and resources used in the classroom. As a member, you don't always get your way, but you can have a say."

Get involved for more than the issue that immediately concerns you, and show the school you're committed to improving education.

CHAPTER 7

Taking Action When Your Child Has a Problem at School

Katie started kindergarten at the neighborhood school with lots of anticipation. Although she was outgoing and loved learning, by mid-October she seemed unhappy at school. Sometimes she complained that she didn't want to go and made comments such as, "Maggie got to be a leader . . . Jack got to help" or "I'm trying to do what the teacher says and be so good, Mommy!"

Her mother, Linda, was puzzled. She asked the teacher if Katie was having a tough time in class, but the teacher responded, "No, she goes overboard to please and to do everything right."

However, Katie continued to be upset about school. Many

mornings when Linda took her to school, she'd cry, begging to stay home. When Linda again talked to her teacher, the teacher insisted that Katie was doing just fine and was one of the best-behaved children in the class.

One Saturday morning in December, Katie burst into tears and asked her mom, "Will you *please* call my teacher and ask her if I can be a helper?"

That week her mom listened closely to everything Katie said, trying to identify the problem. "Is someone in your class bothering you or picking on you?" she asked. "Is something going on at recess? Do you like your teacher? Is there anything at home between Mommy and Daddy that is worrying you?"

A few days later, through their discussions, Linda was able to decipher the problem. Katie had never been chosen to be a "Teacher's Helper." Every day the teacher picked five helpers: Line Leader, Handout Leader, etc. But no matter how hard Katie tried to please her teacher, she was never picked. Her self-confidence had plummeted, and she felt like a failure.

Linda talked with the teacher as soon as possible. "Katie tells me she never gets to be a helper," she said. "What is your criterion for picking helpers?"

The teacher said she chose leaders by pulling five cards from an envelope of names. "I know I must have chosen Katie's card several times," she said. When she showed the stack to Linda, however, they saw that Katie's name wasn't there.

It was just an oversight, but an unfortunate one. Throughout the semester, Katie had tried to be a good student, thinking behavior was the criteria for being picked as a helper. Thus, she had grown increasingly discouraged when she was never chosen regardless of her efforts to please her teacher.

The next day, the teacher brought Katie before the class and said, "Class, I want you to know that I accidentally left Katie's name out of our name cards, and I'm sorry. Katie is going to be a helper today."

Following are several lessons Linda learned from her experience:

- Visit your child's classroom early in the year to know how it operates. During the first week of school, talk to the teacher to find out how she runs her class, how she picks kids for helpers and other special duties, and what kind of rewards and incentives she uses.
- Pursue problems immediately, discover the cause, and find a solution.
- If your child has a misunderstanding with a teacher, as Katie did, be especially selective about choosing his teacher for the following year. It is important that he experiences a positive student-teacher relationship. "I wanted to make sure Katie got the right teacher after the helper incident," Linda said. "A week before enrollment for the next year, my husband and I talked to the principal. I shared with him that Katie is a sensitive child who needs a caring, nurturing teacher. We told him which teacher we felt would meet that criteria."

TAKING INITIATIVE WITH THE SCHOOL

This story and many others I've heard show that when a school problem develops, parents need to communicate with both their child and the teacher. When you see signs of a problem, take the initiative. As Arnold Burron says in *Helping Kids Cope:*

> The actual actions to initiate are not difficult. The difficulty lies in shaking off some of our fears and attitudes

> regarding our own stress level, in being assertive, and in exercising our rights and responsibilities as parents. It is not easy to enter a foreign environment (i.e., the school) and to assert our rights and our child's rights with professionals who "know best." Nevertheless, the stress for us as adults will be easier to manage than the stresses our children might have to face if we abdicate our responsibilities. Even parents who are also teachers do not particularly enjoy taking the initiatives below. It is also true that, all things considered, we would rather ignore potential or actual problems and maybe just "pray them away."
>
> However, after admitting to all of our stresses, let's do as Nehemiah did when he was charged with the task of rebuilding the walls of Jerusalem in the face of an imminent attack by hostile forces. "But we prayed to our God, and because of them we set up a guard against them day and night" (Neh. 4:9). In other words, we must pray because everything depends on God, but we must work as though everything depends on us. Take the initiative. You can reduce your children's stress.[1]

When a problem is identified, most teachers are willing to work together with the parents. However, if the teacher fails to acknowledge the problem, the school may disregard a parent's concerns. The school may even derail your attempts to solve it, and you may need to be persistent.

Younger children often have difficulty verbalizing a problem or identifying its source. They don't want to displease parents and teachers, so they tend to express their problems through behavior.

CHARACTERISTICS OF A CHILD WHO NEEDS ATTENTION

- Has nightmares or sleepwalks
- Is sick in the mornings (your child may develop stomachaches, headaches, or other symptoms on school days. Although the sick feelings and discomfort are real, they often disappear when the child is allowed to stay home)
- Shows anxiety and nervousness
- Has a loss of appetite
- Clings to Mom in the morning, begs not to go to school
- Develops a fear of a specific person or situation
- Withdraws from learning or stops trying
- Is depressed (which in a younger child may be expressed by aggressive, irritating behavior, and in an older child by sadness and fatigue)
- Lacks self-confidence
- Always asks for help before attempting to do things on his own
- Needs lots of praise and reassurance
- Makes excuses for not working in class or not turning in homework
- Is constantly dropping things, daydreaming, and leaving work uncompleted
- Is a late bloomer or delayed developmentally

WHEN THE TEACHER SAYS YOUR CHILD HAS A PROBLEM

Family counselor Ann Benjamin, M.Ed., told me in an interview, "We get hooked into the perfect parent/perfect child myth and think that child development is a smooth uphill trek with no obstacles or hurdles. There are times when our kids are going to have problems and we're going to get notes and calls." Benjamin adds, "We need to try to understand their behavior and help them through the problems."

Poor grades, negative attitudes, and undisciplined behavior can be symptoms of a greater concern. "Obnoxious qualities in kids—misbehaving, failing to cooperate and do schoolwork—are often cries for attention and help," says Guy Doud, 1986 National Teacher of the Year from Brainard High School, Minnesota. Sometimes undetected physical factors are the cause of academic or behavioral problems. Or perhaps a lack of organization, reading difficulties, or turmoil at home is to blame.

FIND OUT YOUR CHILD'S VIEWPOINT

If a teacher has written a note or called about your child, discuss it with him. He may not even be aware of his teacher's feelings. Avoid blaming him or expressing anger. Let him tell his perspective of the story. Ask him:

- "What can you tell me about this?"
- "Is there anything you're aware of that is causing the problem?"
- "Let's talk about your day and the behavior your teacher is talking about."

Maintain open communication with your child about school by spending time with him. Throw a ball, play a game, or walk in the park. Even quiet kids will share their feelings if they are doing something active with you.

DON'T WAIT TO SCHEDULE A CONFERENCE

Sometimes we postpone direct contact with a teacher, thinking the problem will work itself out. However, don't wait for a second note or call. One note or call means the teacher has seen the behavior more than once.

Go to a conference with an attitude of "Let's talk about this." Using this approach, parents teach children how to resolve problems. Begin the meeting with a positive statement, such as, "I'm glad you let me know about this problem" or "I appreciate your concern about my child." Ask the teacher what he thinks the root problem is and listen to him. Until you know the real problem, it's hard to find a solution that works.

ASK THE RIGHT QUESTIONS

Know how to ask the questions that will produce the answers you need. Your inquiries can help the teacher understand and evaluate your child's situation. Following are sample questions:

- How do you see my child functioning in the classroom?
- What is he doing well at school? What are his strengths and weaknesses? In what areas is he making progesss?
- Does he seem happy at school?
- Does he laugh sometimes, get along with others, and relate well to other kids? Is he included in playtime or other activities?
- What have you done about his problem so far?
- How can I help at home?

Go to these meetings with an open mind. Many parents believe their children are perfect and that any problems *must* be caused by the teacher or school. That attitude is *not* helpful. Approach such meetings with a desire not only to express your ideas, but also to gain insight from the teacher.

Complete the meeting by designing a plan of action. Establish steps to be taken at school and home, and schedule a follow-up conference.

EVALUATING YOUR CHILD'S PROBLEMS

You can often learn your child's underlying problems by listening to his teacher's comments about him. Perfectionistic students, undisciplined children, and underachievers exhibit their problems through certain behavior. These types of students need to be approached differently to get their problems solved.

THE PERFECTIONISTIC STUDENT

Cary, a fifth-grader, usually makes top grades, but if she doesn't, she falls apart. She's argumentative and *has* to be right. She has a lot of trouble relating to peers. Cary's argumentativeness may reflect her perfectionism. "Driven kids like Cary use so much energy trying to measure up to their perfectionistic ideals, they don't have much left over for social skills, so they often have difficulty interacting with other children," Ann Benjamin said. She suggests you consider that your child may be a perfectionist if his teacher makes the following comments about him:

- Functions well under pressure
- Is a high performer
- Is nervous, chews his fingers
- Has difficulty interacting with peers
- Is argumentative and cannot accept being wrong
- Challenges the teacher
- Is often angry

When a child is a perfectionist, parents need to consider the message they are sending to that child. Often behind this type of child is a parent with unrealistic expectations. A parent's concentration on the performance of a highly driven child reinforces his self-value as a performer rather than a person. Instead of asking the child, "What did you make on the spelling test?" ask questions such as, "How did recess go today? What are you learning in science now? Who did you sit with at lunch?"

Parents can help the driven child develop non-competitive interests, such as hiking, knitting, jogging, or collecting stamps, coins, or baseball cards. Build a relationship with your child and take time to enjoy each other. Your child's relationship with you is central to his education, motivation, and relationships with others.

Teachers can help by putting this type of child into non-competitive jobs. She can be a good messenger, help in the media center or library, or tutor younger children. A perfectionist needs to be encouraged in expressive areas, such as in music, art, dance, and sports.

THE DISRUPTIVE CHILD

Matt's teacher has written a note to his parents to say that the eight-year-old boy pushes kids around, hits his classmates, and talks back to her. She suggests that they have a conference to discuss his behavior. There may be several reasons for this kind of disruptive behavior. Matt may be frustrated and unable to do his work because of low reading skills. Or he could have too much power at home and needs his parents to set and enforce limits.

Consider that your child may be disruptive if his teacher makes the following comments about him:

- Frequently fights and loses his temper with peers
- Argues a lot
- Is unsuccessful in academics, or is frustrated or bored with the work

- Is disruptive in class
- Is disrespectful and uncooperative with the teacher
- Ignores the teacher when asked to do an assignment
- Turns work in inconsistently

The child with behavior problems at school often needs his parents to set boundaries. He needs Mom and Dad to provide discipline. The adults in his life need to be consistent in dealing with him.

Jess, a first-grader who regularly ignored his teacher, pushed and shoved classmates, and misbehaved at school, said, "Sometimes I feel like my father is pulling my leg in one direction, and my mother is pulling my arm in the other, and I'm in the middle." After his parents established a consistent pattern of discipline at home, his behavior changed dramatically.

If you have a disruptive child, consider your family situation honestly. Has there been major stress or a crisis? Just as the movement of one piece of a mobile makes all the other pieces move as well, since they're all connected, so stress in the family affects not only the adults, but also the children. Declining grades, poor behavior, and underachievement are often signs of inner family turmoil. If there has been a crisis or change in your home, attempt to reestablish stability. Lower the stress level, allow your child to vent his feelings and talk about what concerns him, or grieve with him if there has been the loss of a loved one.

Low grades or a defiant attitude can be a cry for help. Behavior problems may signal overplacement, specific learning problems, or an attention deficit. For example, a first-grade child who is put in a reading group too difficult for him may act out his frustration in bad behavior. Seek help from outside resources, such as the school or family counselor. (See Dr. James Dobson's books *The New Dare to*

Discipline[2] and *Parenting Isn't for Cowards*[3], and Stephen Arterburn and Jim Burns's *Parents Guide to Top 10 Dangers Teens Face.*[4])

THE UNDERACHIEVER

Jenny, a sixth-grader, performs far below her grade level. Most of the time she fiddles with books and pencils, talks to classmates, and passes notes—anything but her schoolwork. Jenny's misbehavior, talking, and note-passing may be masking her real problem—underachieving. Although standardized tests indicate she is capable of making high B's, she forgets homework, and her incomplete work keeps her on the verge of failing. Jenny exemplifies an underachiever.

Consider that your student may be an underachiever if the teacher makes the following comments about him:

- Works at a low level despite high intelligence
- Says he doesn't care about school
- Complains of boredom with school
- Seems to have low self-confidence
- Shows little perseverance for tasks
- Daydreams in class, and forgets assignments and homework

Parents and teachers need to work with underachievers, rather than dismiss their problems as part of a developmental stage. If you have a child like this in the family, set clear, realistic expectations for school and homework. Parents need to listen to what this child is saying. Consider possible factors contributing to underachievement: academic skill problems or mild to severe learning disabilities, chronic poor health, or developmental delays such as hyperactivity or general immaturity. Provide extra support for your child if it is needed.

Explain to your child that homework is his responsibility but that you are willing to help. If Mom has helped him with homework previously, have his father help him. An older child may need a "study buddy," a student from the school or your church youth group who will come once or twice a week to help him get organized, study for tests, and share study tips.

Enrich your child's learning environment outside of the classroom: Provide magazines in his interest areas, go to the library, read aloud as a family, and discuss current events and school projects at dinnertime. (Chapters 9, 10, and 11 offer many ideas for learning beyond the classroom.)

Find your child's "center of learning excitement." John, a bright seventh-grade boy, was doing very poorly in school. When his English teacher discovered he was a World War II history buff, she assigned him a report on that topic. John ended up with a 90-page illustrated book, and discovered in the process he enjoyed doing research and had good writing ability. That year John's grand-father, a TV and radio news broadcaster, took him to his TV station and inspired John to consider a broadcasting career. In high school, he took a community college course in radio/television communication. His underachieving was turned into excelling because his teacher and parents tapped into his interest and skills, and his grandfather mentored him. John is now a successful radio broadcaster and points to junior high as a pivotal time in his life.

HOPE FOR PARENTS OF KIDS WITH PROBLEMS

There is no single cause for the problems a child may encounter at school. But when the teacher says there's a problem and parents respond by supporting their child and working together, they can help him to learn and grow through difficult times. Many kids go through some kind of difficulty during their school years due to developmental delays, crises, health problems, or burnout. But take heart! Often the child who is having problems at eight does great at 12, or the teen who is struggling at 13 sails through at 18.

CHAPTER 8

Helping Your Child Develop Traits That Ensure Success

Karen, a second-grader, isn't flattened by discouragement when she has difficulty learning multiplication tables and doing word problems. She keeps trying, until she finally masters the math concepts.

Dan started school in a new community where classes are larger and he moves to five teachers instead of the one he had in the self-contained fourth-grade classroom back in Minnesota. He'll need to keep hundreds of papers and assignments straight this year and take a lot of initiative in relating to his new teachers and classmates.

When seventh-grader Josh had the flu and bronchitis, forcing him to miss several weeks of school, he wasn't overwhelmed by all the makeup work. Instead, he kept up his enthusiasm and momentum with the support of his mom and dad to keep going and catch up with his classmates.

When Kyser Lough in Simsbury, Connecticut, heard that his dad, Tom, was going to enter the "Iron Horse Boulevard Race," he decided to enter the kids' race. On the morning of the race, Kyser was enthusiastic and set out with the group of young runners. By the time he reached the finish line, 18 kids had dropped out, and he was the *last* of the 72 runners to cross the finish line.

The next day when Kyser's name was listed in the local newspaper as the last runner, his mom and dad were concerned that he'd be teased by kids at school or feel down about it. Instead Kyser said, "Last year, it took me 18 minutes to finish my physical fitness mile at school, but I ran this race in 11 minutes!" His mom and dad said, "What matters is that you *finished* the race and we're proud of you. You really accomplished something!"

Kyser was encouraged for his perseverance, a character quality he'll need to succeed at school and a job someday.

As important as their yellow lunch boxes and number two pencils, your children need to bring some important values and attitudes with them to get the most out of any school experience. They will have many opportunities to learn the three R's of Reading, 'Riting, and 'Rithmetic to progress in school, but they also need to develop R's like Responsibility and Respect and E's like Effort and Enthusiasm, as well as a lot of Perseverance to excel in the classroom and in life. Children who are the most successful at school share these traits and the others discussed in this chapter. Here are some ways we can develop them in our children:

Responsibility. I asked several teachers what their biggest problem was with their sixth-grade students. "Not taking responsibility," they unanimously answered. When parents repeatedly bail kids out when they fail to do their work—enabling, rescuing, and fixing—at a time when students need to be growing more responsible and independent, they don't learn to use their own abilities.

Children who learn responsibility at home are more competent and successful at school. Teachers say they can spot kids who have chores at home. It's important for your child to see himself as a contributing member of the family. Even small jobs, such as washing dishes or feeding the dog, satisfy his desire to feel needed and productive. Teach your child to care for the family pet or to make his own bed, and see that he does it every day. Make sure the chore is age-appropriate: A toddler can pick up his toys, a preschooler can set the table, school-aged children can feed the family pet, clean their rooms, or help with dishes. This helping at home inspires a sense of responsibility. Young people know they aren't helpless, and they can affect their world.

Children who learn responsibility at home are more competent and successful at school.

This sense of being capable also carries over to their school work. When your child has assignments, projects, and homework at school, he will be more able and responsible to carry those out and to do his best.

Homework is, in fact, a tool for developing responsibility and good study habits. "Our children know homework is their responsibility," says Carolyn Curtis. "But they also know I'm available to help them. With our younger son, who is just now beginning to have homework, I still have a lot of input. He doesn't have a choice of studying his spelling words for the test on Friday. The words go up on the refrigerator on Monday, and we help him work on them through the week. I'll be involved helping him build good study habits for several years, but in late junior high, I back off. Our high school daughters are responsible for their own homework, and I rarely have to check on them."

A calendar with space to write down home chores and school assignments helps children develop responsibility. Kids also need to have their own alarm clocks to wake up for school.

Sometimes children fall down on the job and don't get their long-term tasks at school done because the science fair or history project seems overwhelming. Help your child break down tasks and projects into doable "bites." How many days will it take to finish the novel the teacher has assigned—five pages a night or two chapters a week? Brainstorm on science projects and then let your child make a list of needed supplies to make them manageable.

If your child's grade in English was low one marking period and he wants to bring it up, make a poster with stair steps leading to the desired grade, and the three or four steps it will take to achieve the goal. On the first stair write, "Pay attention in class"; on the second, "Do all the reading assignments"; on the third, "Turn homework in on time"; and so on up to the goal.

Respect. Many parents said teaching their children respect for authority helps them learn and succeed at school, and more importantly, it develops foundations for life and their own relationship with God. "Respect and obedience are the two major life skills we want to teach our children," said Roxanne Pierce, an Oakland, Maine, mother. "As Sarah respects me and her dad, she will hopefully in turn respect and obey God, teachers, and others in authority. We feel that being role models to our daughter and son is more important than having a list of rules and will make a longer impression on them. So we show respect and honor their teachers by appreciating them, supporting and listening carefully to them, praying for them, and reading the material they send home."

Judge Randall Hekman, who has seen hundreds of young people in the courtroom, agrees on the importance of respect:

> Parents must teach respect for authority to their children. Many of the kids who come into our courtroom will make recurring visits because their parents always "cover" for them. As soon as the child encounters trouble with school, police or court authorities, one or both parents come to defend the child with such attitudes as: "What he did wasn't so bad. Other kids are doing a lot worse. Why are you picking on my kid?" The child who is so protected by parents—more often a mother—grows up with the feeling that he is immune to laws or rules. He can do as he wants because someone will be there to cover for him. That child will gradually lose his own self-esteem and will become less desirable to society.[1]

When children learn respect for parents at home and respect

other adults in authority, they have a much better chance to relate and learn from their teachers, coaches, and others at school.

Effort. *Effort* means a "strenuous endeavor." Many of the parents I talked with whose children were excelling in school had been very intentional about transferring the value of work, effort, and education to their children.

According to Dr. Sanford Dornbusch of the Stanford Center for the Study of Family & Youth, research studies have shown that the parents of high-achieving Asian children place constant emphasis on *effort* rather than on academic talent or "giftedness," and they encourage their children to work harder. "However, in America we pay too much attention to ability rather than effort, often to the demise of our kids' work habits."

One way to encourage effort is to say to your child, "Of course, you can do better!" And when they do well, make sure they know how pleased you are. "You worked so hard! It's wonderful how much effort you put out for that science project." Also try to positively influence your child's choice of friends by getting families together who share your values of effort and achievement and who emphasize school work. If children have friends who try hard and take pride in their work, they are more likely to excel.

"We've tried to instill in our children that school is their job," said Carolyn Curtis. "Carl has a job in sales, I have a job as a homemaker, and their job is school. They know we expect them to do their best and that their behavior is as important to us as their grades."

"I stress the importance of my children doing their best job every day so they can grow to be all God wants them to be," said Marsha Husk, a California mom. Doing your best and working hard is an important value to transfer to our children that lays a foundation for excellence in their own lives. Joe White and his staff at Kanakuk-Kanakomo Kamps in Branson, Missouri, share with thousands of young people every summer the value of giving 110 percent effort in whatever we do. It's going the extra mile and not taking the easy way out. Scripture tells us "Whatever you do, work at it with all your heart, as working for the Lord" (Colossians 3:23).

How can we help our children strive for excellence in their lives? Ted W. Engstrom, in his book *The Pursuit of Excellence*, suggests that parents must teach their children that God doesn't make mistakes or "average Joes," and that He created each person to be *unique*, with valuable gifts and talents. Parents can help kids strive for excellence with whatever talents God has given them by:

- Being models who put their own talents to work and share their achievements with their children.
- Seeking to know Christ themselves, for He is the true model of excellence.
- Soaking our children's lives with people of excellence—pastors, community leaders, other parents, teachers—and observing them and discovering the qualities in their lives that lead to excellence.[2]

We can also read to our children inspirational stories of athletes and other people (even in history) who gave the extra effort, who strove for excellence, and who didn't give up.

Curiosity and creativity. These qualities are closely linked to a love of learning. How can our homes be places where curiosity and creativity blossom and thrive?

You can boost your child's creativity by storytelling, reading or writing books together, providing art supplies for drawing, or making collages.

Giving your child a big refrigerator box to make a playhouse or blocks and Legos to build a castle stimulates creativity much more than a high-tech toy. A bed sheet can transform a card table into a special "hideaway" or pioneer tent. You can make your own play-dough to create crazy creatures, and encourage your child to make up and tell his own stories.

It's best to limit TV (a passive pastime that stunts creativity) and encourage activity. Beat boredom by providing an "activity center" at home, a table that has drawing paper, crayons, markers, and supplies, materials for collages and crafts, puzzles, and games.

We can encourage children to wonder and think creatively about questions, such as "What could we do with this Styrofoam tray?" or "What are all the ways you could use a toothpick?" If we keep curiosity alive, enthusiasm for learning grows. Saying "Let's look it up" shows your child that you are also curious and still learning and provides a great role model. A parent's attitude of actively encouraging questions and responding with patience, attentiveness, and interest to a child's wondering and exploring goes a long way towards keeping curiosity, creativity, and motivation alive.

Research shows that student achievement rises when parents and teachers ask questions that encourage students to apply, analyze, synthesize, and evaluate information in addition to just recalling facts. Teach your child to think critically and ask questions as she reads:

What made this president or general successful?

What caused this revolution?

What would life be like without the telephone or lightbulb?

Initiative. Let your child learn to do things on his own so he can gain initiative, the energy and drive to take the first step, or learn something totally new. In other words, avoid remaking his bed or rewriting the stories or poems he's written, just so they will look better or sound perfect. Jeff, a fifth-grader, wrote a Valentine letter (along with the rest of his class) for his teacher. He was so proud of it he asked to take it home to show his parents. When he showed it to them, however, his dad got out a pen and started marking and changing it. He gave it back to Jeff and said, "Jeff, you rewrite this before you go back to school." Jeff took the letter, went to his room and rewrote it according to his father's instructions. When he finished, he left it on the kitchen counter and went out to ride his bike.

When children are helped too much by well-meaning parents, they become dependent on Mom and Dad's assistance and figure they can't do without it.

When his mom got home, she took the rewritten letter and started making changes. She even made changes on what Dad had written! When she saw Jeff, she said, "Jeff, you'll need to rewrite this before you go back to school." Jeff rewrote the letter for a second time, but when he gave it to his teacher the next day, he said, "I'm really a crummy writer." Thereafter, Jeff's initiative for writing and other work went down.

When children are helped too much by well-meaning parents, they become dependent on Mom and Dad's assistance and figure they can't do without it. This tears down their self-confidence and initiative to try anything on their own. Young people feel more capable when they hold the ownership to their projects, essays, and homework. So avoid doing it *for* them.

Don't step in, rescue, and take over every time your child struggles with a challenge. Kids are going to run up against problems, and we need to stand by them with the support they need, encouraging them to look for solutions—maybe brainstorming with them and helping them experience some success in doing problem solving—instead of giving all the answers and supplying all the solutions.

This is a tough one for most of us parents. We're older, bigger, we can make a bed faster, and come up with solutions faster. We want to fix every problem for our child. But a healthy practice after a mistake is to ask, "What did you learn from that experience?" in a friendly and supportive, not condemning, way.

If your child really wants to help with a job at home she's considered "too little" for, teach her how to do it—go through the steps, let her try, and you'll be boosting her sense of initiative. Then reward her efforts, even if the dishes are not washed as perfectly or the floor not as shining as if you had done the job.

For example, when he was eight years old, Kyser Lough wanted to learn how to mow the lawn. "Please, let me do it this summer," he pleaded. "I know I can do it!" His mom took time to show him safety precautions, such as wearing protective glasses, not leaning down while the motor was going, etc. She started the mower for him and stayed nearby trimming and edging while he mowed. Not only was he rewarded with some spending money, but he felt like a "capable kid" ready to tackle other challenges.

Enthusiasm and confidence. Kids gain confidence by living in an encouraging atmosphere. We can encourage children by focusing on the *process* of learning, rather than just on the product or the results. (In contrast, pressure builds for a child when we always focus on the score, the win, or the grade.) For instance, if your child is playing on the soccer team and is trying, it's important for you to appreciate and encourage his effort. Encourage him even if the team lost: "You were a team player today. You were out there helping your team." Don't focus only on the results by saying, "Why didn't you get two goals?" or "Why did you miss that goal that you tried to kick into the net?"

If kids are successful in meeting our expectations, they tend to develop more confidence. But if our expectations are always too high for them (if we expect a 98 and are disappointed with an 85; if their sports performance is never good enough; if we always want them to do more than they are capable of), then they tend not to develop confidence. In fact, they become unmotivated or underachievers.

Point out what your child does well, even if this is not school related or academic. Your child's character qualities are important: his loyalty, his spirit of service, his cheerful attitude. Perhaps he is talented in music, in math, art, or writing. The more we can build our child's strengths, the more he can develop confidence. A child must get a sense that his abilities and successes are more important than his failings, and you can help him realize this.

We can also encourage kids with positive words, hugs, smiles, and encouraging notes—maybe stuck in lunch boxes or "pillow notes." By focusing on effort and what they are learning—instead of just the results—you will help your children grow in confidence, and thus motivation.

An enthusiasm for learning develops when Mom and Dad are modeling a love of learning at home. They show interest in what is being taught and learned at school, not just in the grades made.

Enthusiasm also means being excited and fired up about a skill or interest. One way children become motivated about learning is to catch a feeling of enthusiasm about something they want to find out more about or learn how to do. Help your child develop his *own* interests, instead of being rushed from one after-school activity to another that you have chosen. A child who is excited about learning a skill or developing a talent gains momentum to tackle difficult tasks at school. So find out what your child does best and support that with all your might. Kids can develop confidence and skills in drama, sports, fixing lawn mowers, playing the violin, baking, tinkering with computers, swimming, and a host of other hobbies and interests.

Keep alert to what fuels your child's motivation at different ages. At age five it may be whales, snakes, and rocks. But at age 10, your child may be interested in geology, chemistry, or building and launching model rockets if he is a science buff. A child's interests often shows up in his conversation and questions. So go with these interests, even if they aren't interesting to you. Pick up resource books at the library, take an outing related to his interests, and watch for newspaper or magazine articles. If your child's interest is not in an area in which you have any skill, you may be able to find a mentor in your church or neighborhood who can encourage your child.

Perseverance. Perseverance and determination can be more important than IQ, talent, or any other factor. Perseverance is task commitment or persistence to keep on trying in spite of obstacles—an important characteristic that will fuel motivation when times get difficult—and is a key to success in any field. A study of outstanding, talented adults showed that a high IQ, in fact, seems to be less important than specializing in one area of endeavor, persevering, and developing the social skills required to lead and to get along well with others. In sports, home chores, and projects, we need to share with our kids how important it is to be determined to persevere when things get tough, and *to finish what they start.*

Through the years, I've seen that if kids can connect schooling with something in the real world, it can help fire up their desire to learn.

If children develop "stick-to-it-iveness," they can handle failure when it comes and bounce back. Think of the skater who falls down in an important competition and then gets back up and goes on to finish her performance, or the scientist who tries and fails hundreds of times in his search for a vaccine for a disease. Teach your child that making mistakes is part of learning, and share stories, books, and newspaper clippings of people who persevered and overcame obstacles and failure in their lives.

I remember my mom and dad telling us, "If at first you don't succeed, try, try again!" You can help your child learn perseverance when you say:

"That's a long assignment, but stick with it and you'll get the problems done."

"We're so proud of you for hanging in there with your soccer team and trying so hard even though you haven't had a winning season."

"Press on; you're going to make it!"

"You wanted to take guitar lessons, and you'll need to see them through all year."

There are also activities and experiences that build perseverance and determination: planting and caring for a garden, learning to sew, woodworking, music lessons, swimming on a swim team, learning to play tennis.

Aspirations and goals. The ability to set and follow goals (both short- and long-term) is a trait that separates high-achieving kids from less successful ones. Through the years, I've seen that if kids can connect schooling with something in the real world, it can help fire up their desire to learn. When a child has goals and aspirations, he is much more motivated in the classroom and can surmount problems along the way toward his goals.

"The typical young person lacks confidence about who he is and where he fits—he doesn't have dreams," says Jim Dodgen, career counselor.

Dan, a young man I've known since he was seven years old, greatly admired his dentist and was fascinated with the instruments and techniques he observed on his visits to the dentist's office. He decided that someday, he was going to be a dentist. It wasn't an easy path. Because he hadn't developed strong study skills in the small rural high school he attended, he had difficulty with the college predental courses. In fact, his grades were not promising and chances looked dim.

He changed to a smaller university and plowed into his studies, determined that someday he was going to be a dentist. Before he was admitted to dental school, however, he had to spend an extra year in college to get his grades up. On his final exams at the end of his freshman year of dental school, he missed passing by only one-tenth of a point and thus had to repeat the whole first year of dental school. He continued to work hard and graduated from dental school. Today, he is a successful dentist with a growing practice. It hasn't been an easy road, but those youthful goals motivated him with perseverance and drive along the way.

In contrast to Dan, many young people lack direction and purpose. "The typical young person lacks confidence about who he is and where he fits—he doesn't have dreams," says Jim Dodgen, career counselor.

"If you're a skeptic, you might be thinking that dreams—real dreams—are reserved for those few people with special gifts or talents," he continues. "In truth, by God's design, each of us possesses a unique combination of skills, interests, and values—the stuff dreams are made of. And just like those Bible characters in the parable of the talents (Matthew 25:14-30), God expects us to use our talents to the best of our ability, not hide them under some rock."[3]

By fifth to eighth grades and especially in high school, children need to be afire with goals and dreams for the future. Here are some ways we can help develop goals and aspirations in young people:

- Provide a broad base of experience by taking your children on outings to interesting places. Encourage kids to have hobbies, pursue their interests, and join clubs.
- Appreciate children's skills, talents, and character qualities and give them opportunities to use and develop them at church, home, and school.
- Read biographies of great men and women, such as Clara Judson's *Abraham Lincoln;* Ben Carson's *Gifted Hands*, about how he overcame an impoverished childhood to become a leading surgeon; or Joni Eareckson Tada's *Joni*, the story that tells about the accident that

left her paralyzed, how her faith in God grew, and how she became a fine artist, author, and advocate for the physically handicapped. As I read Clara Barton's biography over and over in my growing up years, I remember being inspired by her courage and sense of purpose. Missionaries' stories also make fascinating reading. Save articles and share with your children about people who have interesting callings and careers.

- Let children see different careers, ministries, and occupations. At a court hearing, for instance, they will see several vocations at work: a judge, court reporter, attorneys, bailiff, etc. At an inner-city ministry or shelter they see people serving and using interpersonal, administrative, and counseling skills. Encourage them to ask people about their jobs and visit job sites to gain understanding. Take your child to work with you. Part-time work, summer employment, or volunteer work also provides opportunities to find out about careers. Our daughter thought she wanted to be a nurse and served as a candy striper in a large hospital's I.C.U. After that experience, she decided she only wanted to work in the baby nursery! When Kim, a high school junior, had a chance to work on Saturdays for a graphic artist, she decided she wanted to major in graphic arts.

Adults and parents in churches can take the time to share their career experiences and mentor young people. At our church, different adults shared each week at the junior high youth group about their ministry or career. They told how God had equipped them and was working in their lives and work. Boy Scouts of America has a fine career program, Explorer Scouts, for boys and girls, ages 14 to 21. Parents can call the local scout office for information. For example, the Veterinarian Explorer group in Denver, Colorado, meets twice a month with volunteer specialists in the field. This is a great boost to the aspirations of the young people who participate.

As we develop the traits of responsibility, respect, curiosity, creativity, initiative, enthusiasm, confidence, and perseverance at home, we can help kids get the best foundation and education they can to meet the challenges that lie ahead. We will also be helping them develop values that they will use in their families, relationships, jobs, and ministries. In the next chapter, we'll look at how to help children develop the vital organizational skills they need to succeed in school.

CHAPTER 9

Helping Your Child Develop Organizational and Study Skills

Disorganization is a leading cause of failure, discouragement, and lack of motivation. On the other hand, organization goes a long way toward making your child a success in the classroom.

At age 13, Ashley entered a public junior high after attending a small Christian school. She was quickly overwhelmed with the homework, handing in her work late and in general being disorganized. Her grades plummeted. Concerned about her changed performance, her parents found Ashley a college-aged "study buddy" to help her organize her notebook and keep track of assignments. The young woman gave Ashley some tips for success in the classroom and helped her study for tests. As Ashley became more organized, she began to enjoy her classes more, and her grades improved.

Kids like Ashley, who forget homework assignments or misplace textbooks, often have difficulty concentrating. Organized students generally do better in school, and organizational skills become increasingly important as students advance through the grades.

Some children are natural organizers—they color-categorize their socks in their drawers and keep all the hangers in their closet pointed in the same direction. However, many children need help keeping assignments, books, and papers straight. (It is *especially important* for children with learning problems to have someone help them be organized.)

Following are some home and school organizers that will decrease anxiety, increase success at school, and help your child avoid tears over low grades, lost papers, and books.

- Family calendar. With poster board, make your own calendar for the month. (Laminate it with clear contact paper.) Mark activities, such as band concerts, PTA meetings, Bike Safety Saturday, due dates for science projects, church activities, and birthdays.
- Child's calendar. Place a smaller version of the family calendar in your child's room as a visual reminder. The schedule will help your child set goals and complete projects in several steps rather than doing them at the last minute. He can record his soccer practice, golf lessons, youth group retreat, vacation days, Boy Scout camp, and the due date for his book report.
- Family bulletin board. Display your children's drawings,

book reports, creative stories, and math papers on corkboard somewhere in the house. Attach notes of encouragement, saying "I know you'll do great on your spelling test!"

- School box and bag. Learning organization begins in kindergarten. Give each child a school bag or backpack and designate a certain place by the door for him to put it when he comes home from school. Place coats, gloves, and hats in the school box so that everything is ready for the next day.
- Desk and study area. Here are some materials your child will need at a desk:

pen, pencils with erasers, markers
loose-leaf notebooks containing dividers and pockets for handouts
scissors, ruler, scotch tape
stapler or paper clips
a dictionary, thesaurus, and spelling guide
a good light
a comfortable chair
a place to keep materials
a place to post a school planning calendar
a pad to list goals and check off accomplishments
3 x 5 index cards for flash cards
a file folder for tests and homework
a typewriter or computer
a tape recorder with blank tapes
a kitchen timer to mark study time and breaks

The home study place also needs to be quiet and away from the television.

HOUSEHOLD ROUTINES

Routines at home provide the structure kids need to stay on track during the school year. "A home without ritual is a home with a high prospect of homework problems," says Faith Clark, Ph.D. "Structure and ritual, including regular meal- and bedtime, and the bedtime story, form the foundation for learning."[1]

Have a morning routine for waking up and preparing for school. (Your child should have his own alarm clock.) Serve nutritious breakfasts and eat dinner as a family at a regular time.

Create a routine for doing chores, giving each child a list of weekly responsibilities (keep room clean, feed dog, etc.). Supply family members with a list of Saturday chores where each person is assigned certain jobs. When the tasks are done, celebrate with a visit to the park or the ice cream shop. The routine of regular homework times builds good study habits and is important to build into your family's day.

A TIME AND A PLACE TO STUDY

"It takes about four to six days to formulate a habit pattern for a school-age student," says Dr. Wanda Draper, professor of psychiatry at the University of Oklahoma Medical School. "Have him study in the same place at the same time each day." After your child develops a habit of daily study, he won't debate whether or not to do his homework.

Pattern setting is important here. Our minds become accustomed to daily patterns. As adults, we don't make a decision to brush our teeth each morning and evening; we do it out of habit. Similarly, we don't want our children making decisions about whether or not to do homework—they should do it naturally. We can start a child out with a positive pattern of studying in the same place and time (especially at the beginning of the school year), and he can have a more effective study or homework time.

When you teach your child to brush his teeth properly, you are involved in the process at first, but after a while you merely check to make sure he is brushing consistently and to give gentle reminders when he forgets. Then comes the wonderful time when it becomes second nature and he does it on his own without thinking. Building study habits is much the same; it takes time and patience, but it is a process worth learning and internalizing!

When should a child study? At what times of the day is his attention span greatest? How late should he study? For most children, having a snack after school and then time to unwind and play outside before sitting down to do homework works well. If he has homework in two subjects, he can do one assignment before dinner and one after. Or he may prefer to get all his homework done before the evening meal so there will be a time afterwards to play a board game or read as a family.

Decide on a time with your child and post it to remind him. If assigned homework is completed before the time is up, the remaining time could be used to read, work on long-range projects, or review for an upcoming test.

If you ask your child if he has any homework today, he's likely to say "No, I don't think so," meaning that he doesn't have an assignment due the following day. However, he may have several large projects due at the end of the week. He needs to develop the habit of daily study even if he has nothing due the next day. A better question to ask your child when he comes home from school might be, "Which subject are you planning on starting first, reading or math?"

Typically children in the fifth grade or below can study 15

minutes at a time, take a five-minute break, and then study for another 15 minutes. "If a young student takes more than a 10-minute break, his mind may begin to wander and he will have difficulty returning to his work," Dr. Wanda Draper told me in an interview. With a five-minute break to get a drink of water or an apple or play with the dog, the body can relax, but the subconscious mind continues to work on the material, according to Dr. Draper. An older student can effectively study and concentrate for 30-minute intervals interspersed with five-minute breaks.

Study time is best utilized if telephone calls, loud music, and the television do not distract your child, allowing him to fully concentrate on a specific task, book, or project.

Help your child make a checklist of tasks for each study session and estimate the amount of time needed to complete them. Cross off the tasks listed on the sheet when the work is completed.

Help him break big tasks into small, manageable jobs. Make each small task a goal for a study session. For example, if he has a 20-page chapter in history to read by Monday, he can read four pages each day during the week and review the chapter over the weekend.

NO MORE HOMEWORK HASSLE WITH MY TEEN!

After my friend Linda's teenage son brought home a low progress report for the third time, she decided to take action. Linda placed a "sign-in" sheet on the refrigerator. Instead of withholding privileges, she helped her son, Paul, take control of his homework time. He was to study for 90 minutes a day and record his homework hours on the "sign-in" sheet, breaking up his study time into 15- to 30-minute increments as he wished. The time sheet gave him guidance and helped him develop responsibility. He didn't feel as if he were being punished; instead, he felt he had the freedom to succeed! Paul made his best GPA that semester. This method has also benefited other high school students. Following are some tips for making it work:

If your student doesn't have any assignments to complete during his study time, he can either outline a chapter or read ahead. If he has a chance to read the material *before* attending the class covering it, he will retain and understand more of the information.

It is helpful for the older student to rewrite, review orally, or correct lecture notes on a daily basis. He can make any needed corrections while the information is still fresh in his mind. Being exposed to the information helps him process and retain what he must learn.

"BUT TEACHER, THE DOG ATE MY HOMEWORK": KEEPING UP WITH DAILY ASSIGNMENTS

When I taught school, I heard many interesting excuses for homework not being done, such as:

My dog (or cat) ate my homework.

The computer ate my homework.

My little brother finger-painted on it.

Mom spilled spaghetti sauce all over it.

Students who regularly complete homework assignments do better academically. An assignment notebook or calendar is a necessary tool for students to write down assignments so they can keep up in class. Long-term assignments like book reports and projects can be recorded on the calendar at home. A notebook with space for daily entries works well. A weekly calendar sheet with blocks for each subject and day of the week may help a younger child. Photocopy this calendar and staple it to the front of your child's notebook each week. He can take it to class to help him remember to write down his assignments. For extra accountability, have the child's teacher initial the sheet.

As you teach your child organizational skills, he will grow increasingly responsible, confident, and independent.

Our daughter Alison used a calendar sheet throughout elementary and middle school to stay on track in her classes. In high school, she used a small, daily appointment book to write down short- and long-term assignments, track meets, ballet classes, and other activities.

Andy came to his English class with papers from four different classes stuck in his books; he didn't know where his workbooks were and he was failing everything. Linda, his tutor, took him to the store and bought six plastic binders, one for each class. She added dividers and a clear zipper bag with pens and pencils; these, she color-coded and labeled. Inside each binder were the divisions: assignment sheets, class notes, homework, tests, etc. Linda helped Andy use his new system, and after a few weeks he became so organized he even earned extra points in one class for having his parents sign his assignment sheet every Tuesday night. He was getting all his homework done and even kept his coat, shoes, and football equipment in better order. By the end of the semester, his grades came up to all B's.

As you teach your child organizational skills, he will grow increasingly responsible, confident, and independent.

DOING HOMEWORK USING A CHILD'S UNIQUE LEARNING STYLE

Another key to helping your child succeed in public school is to help him use his unique learning style, which may be visual, kinesthetic-tactile, auditory, or a combination. After our teenage son was stymied by trying to memorize a long poem in archaic early 1800s language, I suggested he read the whole poem on a blank tape, then use it to practice whenever he was in the car. For several days, he played it and recited along with it on the way to school, sports practice, and his part-time job. By tapping into his learning strengths—his auditory and verbal channels—he became successful at an otherwise frustrating and difficult assignment.

You can discover your child's learning style by observing his eye movements, the way he tackles problems and expresses himself, and his likes and dislikes. Then adjust homework assignments to his learning style. If a homework lesson is visual (such as reading a chapter from his history book), you can make it auditory by reading it aloud together or letting your child recite it onto a blank tape (which he can later use for review).

The kinesthetic-tactile learner likes to try things out, is physically active, can ride a bike earlier than anyone in the neighborhood—but often fidgets in class and may have trouble learning to read. He needs to take a hands-on approach to math, science, and other subjects. He's helped by a big blackboard at home on which he can rehearse and practice spelling words, and maybe can even teach you the information. He often needs the most help organizing and should be allowed to be active while reviewing (such as bouncing a basketball in the driveway as he says his multiplication tables).

Auditory learners love to talk, need clear oral directions, and are never too old to be read to. They answer the teacher's questions readily in class. Their learning is aided by having a study partner to quiz material with, and by using a tape recorder to make their own study tapes.

The visual learner has a good memory for faces, numbers, and facts, is often quiet, and rarely volunteers answers in class. He loves puzzles and is very observant of details. Spelling comes easily for him because it involves visualization. This type of learner works best from a list of jobs or assignments, enjoys working alone, and can stay focused on a task if his desk is neat and organized.

Once you help your children understand their learning style, they become more active learners, can do homework more efficiently, and enjoy school more.

For more information on learning styles, see my book *Unlocking Your Child's Learning Potential*.[2]

CHAPTER 10

Helping Your Child with Reading and Writing

Because Susan's children rarely read the classics in public schools, she had them read Beatrix Potter and A. A. Milne at home at a young age. Later, she discovered that if she wanted them to read books, such as *Five Little Peppers*, *Little Women*, *Tom Sawyer*, *Kidnapped*, *Ivanhoe*, *Moby Dick*, and *The Scarlet Letter*, she would have to introduce them to these books as well. Consequently, she assigned them reading material and book reports in addition to their schoolwork. Of course, there were the inevitable complaints: "No one else in my class has to read these books!" But Susan stuck with her plan despite the objections.

A few years later she received a thank-you letter from her oldest daughter. Ann was exempted from college freshman English by taking Advanced English in her senior year of high school. She qualified to take an advanced placement test in English literature for sophomores. Out of the 30 students who took the test, only two were able to complete the exam, and Ann was the only one to earn an A.

Ann believes her mom's home reading program enabled her to succeed on the test. Her younger sister and brother are following the same reading program. Her brother, Josh, has multiple handicaps but still has become an avid reader. The secret? Reading classics, memorizing poetry and Scripture, limiting television, and developing a family library. Says Susan, "We underestimate our children's ability and deny them so much by not giving them quality reading."

A recent *Reader's Digest* article showed how even the best students get an inferior education, full of mediocre "age-appropriate" reading assignments. The author said that if we feed students the literary equivalent of junk food, they'll end up with a lackluster command of English. To counteract this insufficient education, you can supplement your child's reading at home. (See "Can't-Miss Treasures: A Supplemental Home Reading List" in Appendix I to get you started.)

Your child's reading level significantly impacts his success at school. Early in their school years, students are categorized into high, middle, and low learning levels, often according to their reading ability. Since these labels are often difficult to remove, it is important that we help our children enter school well prepared to read.

HELPING YOUR CHILD READ

Reading is the most important academic skill because *almost 90 percent of all school work requires reading.* If your child becomes a good reader, many learning and school problems can be prevented.

Role modeling is the best way to get your child to read. If you let him see you reading for fun and enjoyment, you will build a *love of reading*. Go to the public library with him. If you notice him reading a book, ask him to let you read it too. Later, discuss it with him.

Ask your child's teacher what kind of reading program she uses at school. Most teachers use a combination of several methods to teach reading:

- Look-say method: a rote word memory system based on visual cues (mastering words by examining the nearby drawing) and sight-word recognition (words that appear over and over in text).
- Intensive phonics: a method focused on learning letters, blends, and syllable sounds.
- Eclectic phonics: a combination of phonetic methods according to the child's ability, which may combine visual cues, sounds of words, and parts of words.
- Word Attack: another name for phonics skills.
- "Whole language:" a literature-based reading and writing program.

Most public school reading programs use the "look-say" method despite evidence that many children have difficulty learning to read without a strong phonics program. If your child is not getting phonics training in the classroom, provide it at home. An excellent resource on reading methods is *Why Johnny Still Can't Read: A New Look at the Scandal of our Schools*, by Rudolf Flesch.[1]

About 20-30 percent of children have some kind of reading difficulty, but only 2 percent of the population are truly dyslexic. Letter and word reversal is common with first- and second-graders but only persists with dyslexics.[2] Don't accept a dyslexic label on your child even if he has some reading difficulties. Start a home reading program, have his reading skills evaluated, or get him a tutor, but *make sure he learns to read well.*

For children with dyslexia, one of the most successful methods of teaching reading is "Alphabetic Phonics." Pioneered by Dr. Samuel T. Orton, the program is based on a multisensory approach that teaches reading, handwriting, and spelling together with auditory, visual, and kinesthetic methods. Many teachers in the United States have been trained in Alphabetic Phonics, and you can get information from the Orton Dyslexia Society (1-800-222-3123) for tutoring or schools in your community.

EVALUATING YOUR CHILD'S READING SKILLS

Here are some suggestions to help you evaluate your child's reading ability.

- Oral reading—Does he read aloud without stumbling over words? Can he sound out unfamiliar vocabulary?
- Comprehension—Does he understand what he has read? Can he draw logical conclusions?
- Book selection—Does he choose books that challenge him?
- Spelling—Even if your child is a poor speller, do his mistakes reflect the phonetic pronunciation of a word?
- Auditory processing—Can he follow written and verbal instructions?
- Interest—Does he express apathy? Does he complain of tiredness connected with schoolwork or homework?
- Physical activity—Does your child move constantly when reading?

If the answer is no to the first five questions and yes to the last two, your child may have a reading problem. You can help him by reading with him at home. All children need to be read to, especially those having trouble with comprehension. By reading aloud to your child, you model the expression, phrasing, and flow of a passage. Remember children are never too old to be read to!

Read-aloud time should be enjoyable, relaxed, and informal. If possible, parents, grandparents, and siblings should read to the child. Choose different places for reading, such as in front of the fire or under a big tree in the backyard. Read aloud while waiting for the doctor, when your child is ill, at bedtime, or while traveling.

Many parents read to their children in the preschool years, then depend on the schools to complete the reading education. However, in most elementary classrooms, each child may get only a few minutes daily to practice reading aloud. And he may only get seven or eight minutes of reading silently—*not enough time* to become a fluent reader!

LISTENING TO YOUR CHILD READ ALOUD

Following are some tips to help you help your child read aloud.

- Review the section or story he is going to read, and define and pronounce any new or difficult words *before* he starts reading. If he can't sound out a word or figure it out by the context of the sentence within four or five seconds, help him.
- Return to the problem words after reading the chapter or section.
- Pay attention to what your child is reading aloud to you. Kids can usually tell when your mind is wandering.
- Choose fun books, read with lots of drama (even encourage your child to use different voices and tones for different characters—which helps comprehension—and talk about what you are reading).

- Be supportive, encouraging, and positive when your child reads aloud.
- Use rewards to help motivate children to read. Offer a game-playing time with Mom or Dad, a treat, or a bubble bath as a gift.
- Set realistic time limits and be sensitive to your child's age and development. Often a slow or reluctant reader's eye muscles and attention skills don't allow for prolonged reading sessions. The typical first-grader has an attention span of 20 minutes.

ENCOURAGING THE PRESCHOOL TO ELEMENTARY CHILD'S READING

Here are some suggestions for parents of preschoolers.

- Place a label on your child's toy box, closet, drawers, towels, and special possessions. Show him that words have meaning and can be used to identify his belongings.
- Help him read words around the home, in the grocery store, or on the road, such as recipes, newspapers, cereal boxes, billboards, and road signs.
- Make an alphabet book with your child. Put a different letter and photo on each page. For example, the "D" page could include a photo of your child with his dog. If he has a special interest in science, you can help him make a "Bird and Bug" or "Ocean" alphabet book.
- Speak to your child in clear, complete sentences.
- Give him a children's Bible with his name embossed on the cover. A personal Bible can boost his reading and spiritual development and inspire him to memorize verses.

- Encourage him to tell stories. Storytelling builds concentration, sequencing skills, comprehension, and vocabulary. Storytelling also strengthens communication skills, which are extremely important in today's society since many parents and kids spend more time watching TV than talking with one another.
- Play word games in the car or tell rhymes, limericks, tongue twisters, and riddles. Select a category such as "fruit" and have each player name a fruit until the list has been exhausted. To make the game more difficult, select a category and a letter. For example, have the players name all the animals that begin with "S."
- Memorize Bible verses and poetry. Even small children can memorize short verses and enjoy it; memory greatly improves with practice.
- Build a home library. Include books you have read aloud on trips or around the fireplace. Buy books at local book fairs, new and used bookstores, and school book clubs. Have a special shelf for library books so they can be kept separate and are easily accessible to return to the library.
- On snowy or rainy days when boredom or "cabin fever" sets in, let your child make a "tent" with a sheet over a card table. Throw some pillows on the floor along with a new book to read in his "hideaway."

HELPING THE MIDDLE SCHOOL CHILD READ

Suggestions for helping your middle school child include:

- Select books for your child that promote biblical values and feature strong Christian characters. For example, have your child read *The Courage of Sarah Noble* by Alice Dagliesh, *Little House on the Prairie* by Laura Ingalls Wilder, *Caddie Woodlawn* by Carol Brink, and *Out of the Blue* by Orel Hershiser.

- Older children enjoy hearing a chapter of a book each night and anticipating the next episode. A series, such as C.S. Lewis' *The Chronicles of Narnia* or Madeline L'Engle's *Time Quartet*, works well. If your child particularly enjoys one author, find other books by that author, and encourage her to write the author.
- Give gift certificates for a bookstore to your child for his birthday.
- Have an SSR (Silent Sustained Reading) time as a family. Don't forget to turn off the television and stereo.
- Subscribe to a magazine that addresses your child's interests. For a sports fan, get *Sports Illustrated;* for a car enthusiast, *Road & Track;* for an outdoorsman or Boy Scout, *Field & Stream* or *Boy's Life*. *Brio*, *Breakaway*, *Clubhouse*, and *Clubhouse Jr.* (published by Focus on the Family) are excellent magazines for young people. Encourage your child to read the daily newspaper, clip out articles of special interest, and discuss current events, sports, community news, and interesting people in the news.
- If your child is studying something at school in science, history, or another subject he finds interesting, pick up a book on the same subject from the library.
- Avoid putting a television in your child's bedroom! When "boredom" sets in, encourage reading for entertainment.

WAYS TO SPARK OR BOOST YOUR CHILD'S READING AT ANY AGE

We can stimulate our child's reading interest at any age by capitalizing on his interests. Observe the types of books he selects at the library. Does he look for books on sports or science fiction? Develop his interests and encourage him to start hobbies. Many hobbies, such as collecting baseball cards or stamps, involve reading.

Share books with him, too. Tony was an active 13-year-old in junior high. He didn't enjoy reading, but he did like science. As a child, he would stand in the backyard at night and gaze at the stars—"Look at that meteor!" he'd say. "Look at that constellation!" He was very curious about astronomy, but in school he didn't like to do homework and his grades showed it. He made C's and D's even though he was bright.

One day, Tony came home with a science fiction book his teacher had recommended. *Dune* told about a group of people who lived on a desert planet. Tony was excited about reading the book, and his father seized the opportunity to read it at the same time so they could discuss the story together. Their relationship began to change as they shared their opinions and read other books together. Tony's attitude, behavior, and grades improved, and he continued to talk to his dad about things he wouldn't have discussed previously.[3]

HELPING THE STRUGGLING READER

If your child is struggling with reading, he needs your help.

- Check out books from the library that interest your child and are somewhat below his level. With easier books, he can increase his reading speed and proficiency while building confidence.

- Watch videos or movies, such as *Black Beauty* or *Anne of Green Gables*, to encourage a reluctant reader to tackle the book version.
- Buy or rent computer reading games. These can improve reading skills for the math-oriented or kinesthetic learner.
- Give your child a bedside light and a stack of books for his own quiet reading time before "lights out."
- Provide a taped version of the story or book so your child can listen while following along silently.

HELPING YOUR CHILD WRITE

Writing skills affect your child's learning and achievement in *every* subject. If he writes well, he will be a more successful student. But he needs your help with school writing, and he needs to do some "home writing" to become proficient.

Many students get stuck trying to decide on a topic. They use all their homework time staring at a blank sheet of paper and become discouraged, saying, "I can't think of anything to write."

When a topic is assigned, help your child brainstorm and write down the ideas. Then he can sort through them and choose a few from which to make an outline. Help him prewrite the story by telling it verbally, then writing the first draft quickly in one sitting, getting all of his ideas on paper. Let him set the draft aside for one or two days, then have him edit his work, checking for misspelled words, grammatical errors, and poor sentence structure. Have him write a second draft.

Encourage your writer to read the paper aloud or tape record and listen to it before revising. Ask thoughtful questions that focus on ideas and content. Avoid harsh criticism. Find something positive to say about his word choice, sentences, or some other aspect of his paper. Although you may advise him about a word or sentence or suggest a change, he needs to make the correction himself and thus retain ownership of the writing project.

Show interest in your child's work by keeping the best stories, reports, and essays in a writing folder after they are displayed on the family bulletin board or refrigerator. Reviewing his old papers can help him see his improvement.

EVALUATING YOUR CHILD'S WRITING SKILLS

Although children mature according to their own time clocks, when given the time, encouragement, and materials to write, the normal student will progress through certain developmental stages:

Kindergarten and first grade: The child tends to write in the same way he plays blocks—for the sake of the activity, rather than for the final product. He rehearses a story by drawing and talking. He usually invents his own spelling and can often produce delightful poems and stories.

Second and third grades: The child learns to use more conventional spelling, punctuation, and capitalization. He writes letters and stories with a plot, sequence, and dialogue.

Fourth through sixth grades: Vocabulary continues to build so that by fifth grade the child can usually spell most basic words. He revises for better meaning and mechanics. He writes stories several pages long with conflict, characterization, and dialogue. He learns to take notes, use reference materials such as the dictionary and thesaurus, and write factual stories and reports.

Seventh through ninth grades: The typical junior high writer organizes and composes essays, stories, and reports. Writing flows more easily, the student's vocabulary is wider, and he is more descriptive.

Learning to edit and revise his first draft into a polished final copy will hopefully become a normal part of his writing process.

Tenth through 12th grades: The high school student gains practice in writing well-organized expository papers, and precise, descriptive, and narrative essays. He learns to write a research paper using library resources. In the process, he takes notes, makes outlines and footnotes, takes references, and makes a bibliography. By the end of high school, his writing skills should be solid and competent.

HELPING THE PREREADER AND KINDERGARTNER WRITE

There are many ways you can encourage younger children to write. For instance:[4]

- Provide paper, markers, crayons, and other materials for drawing and painting to encourage your preschooler's writing skills. Encourage your child to discuss his drawings. Ask, "Can you tell a story about this picture?" or "What is the girl doing?" Research shows that the best writers did lots of drawing as young children.[5]
- Have your child find a picture of a word he likes, cut it out, and glue it to a colored index card. On the back of the card, he can print the word. Put the card in a "word box" to be reviewed in the future.
- Put pencils, order pads (the kind used in restaurants), envelopes, and clipboards near your children's play toys and costumes. While playing hospital, restaurant, or office, they can write receipts and make sales slips. When playing post office, they can write letters and address and "mail" them in their own homemade mailbox.

- Make your own book. Prewriters can dictate stories to their parents. Covers can be made of cardboard covered with contact paper, and pages can be sewn or stapled.

  For an "All About Me" book, your child can choose 10 pictures from infancy to the present, put them in chronological order, and glue in a scrapbook. Your child can dictate to you the story of what is happening in each picture or write in "invented spelling." Another book can include a series of family pictures of a special outing with the child's written story below.
- Send encouragement notes. Children love to receive notes in their lunch boxes or on their pillows. Even if they are too young to read very well, they will work to figure out the message. Then encourage your child to write notes to surprise family members.

HELPING THE ELEMENTARY CHILD WRITE

Here are some suggestions that can help make your elementary child a better writer:

- Have your child write letters. Supply bright stationery, envelopes, stickers, addresses, and stamps for your child. When traveling, have him send postcards to friends, family, and favorite teachers.
- Have your child write thank-you notes.
- Provide note pads for making lists of science project or camping trip supplies, Christmas or birthday wishes, favorite books, daily chores, school assignments, and summer activity ideas.
- Make maps and write directions to a friend's house. Make a map of your neighborhood with your child's

house, school, stores, landmarks, and street names.

- Encourage your child to make original cards for birthdays, Valentine's Day, or holidays and write his own greeting or poem. Have him design his own birthday party invitations. Supply construction paper and stickers.
- Let your child use a word processor or computer. If he's a poor speller, then "spell check" software will be helpful. Do family writing projects on the computer. For example, compose a family Christmas letter with your child.

HELPING THE MIDDLE SCHOOL CHILD WRITE

As writing assignments become more difficult, there are many ways you can help your young writer.

- Encourage middle school children to write about their interests. John was fascinated by the space program. He went to the library for books, made a scrapbook of drawings of space shuttles, explained the equipment, and wrote on the future of NASA for his school report. Mary loved Great Danes, so she did research on them, wrote to veterinary schools in the state, and made stationery with her own Great Dane logo.
- Have your child interview grandparents and relatives and make a family history book. He can write out questions beforehand, take notes, and tape record the interview.
- Write notes, such as, "Don't forget to feed the cat!" or "Good luck on your science test!" to give encouragement, enhance a busy family's communication, and encourage your child to write.
- Get a pen pal for your child. Through lively correspondence with a child from a foreign country, he learns how

people in other cultures live. Ask your church mission board for the name of a child from a missionary family with whom your child can correspond. Or you can get a pen pal for your child by sending a self-addressed, stamped envelope to International Friendship League, Department A, 22 Batterymarch, Boston, MA 02109. Another source is World Pen Pals, 1690 Como Avenue, St. Paul, MN 55108.

- Encourage journal-keeping. Besides providing writing practice, a journal is a great outlet for expressing feelings. Buy a cloth-bound blank book in which your child can record his feelings and events. Remember to respect your child's privacy and avoid "journal snooping."

HELPING THE STRUGGLING WRITER

Sometimes children struggle with writing assignments or get stuck in the middle of writing about a topic. Some children have trouble writing in complete sentences, or may run two sentences together even in junior high. Here is one way to help the struggling writer:

Increase the reading and writing your child does at home through activities, such as those suggested in this chapter. Research shows that the most important ingredient in writing-skill development is the home environment. Too much television and too little reading at home have a negative effect on children's writing ability, no matter what reforms and great programs are going on at school.

CHAPTER 11

Helping Your Child with Science, Math, Geography, and History

It was Thursday evening, and Tom Lough was sitting in the living room with his eight-year-old son Kyser at his side. They had just finished reading the encyclopedia entry about dinosaurs for a science project when Kyser found a diagram of a dam.

"Hey, Dad, look at this!" Kyser exclaimed. "This dam is just like the one we saw on the Colorado River. I'll never forget how the water sounded when it poured over the other side of the dam."

Kyser flipped back a page and found another diagram of a dam. "Dad, let's read about this," he suggested.

"Okay, son," Tom said as they looked at the pictures together.

"Hey, Dad, we could build a model of a dam just like this one!"

With excitement, Kyser listened to his dad read about dams and then went to the store with him to get the needed supplies. That Saturday they began working on the project. After several evenings of work and much trial and error, the water wheels were working.

Kyser and his father invited his mother to see their final product. She was so impressed that she suggested they videotape the working dam and send a copy of the tape to the grandparents. Two sets of proud grandparents watched the tape and then wrote to Kyser to compliment him on his hard work.

HELPING YOUR CHILD WITH SCIENCE

Because science is one of the weakest subjects for American students, parents need to stimulate their child's interest in the subject with hands-on projects. If your child's science class consists of worksheets and textbook exercises, provide supplemental projects at home to make the subject come alive. You can also assist the teacher in getting science kits and activities for the classroom.

Especially in the early elementary years when children's attitudes about science are being formed, it's vital for us to stimulate their interest in science with hands-on projects—from collecting and pressing bright autumn leaves to stargazing in the backyard with a star map or watching a caterpillar grow a cocoon and hatch into a beautiful butterfly.

In all science projects and activities your child does at school and at home, remember: modeling matters! Parents' demonstrating positive attitudes about science has a lot to do with a child's attitude in the classroom and can prevent "science anxiety." Even if we aren't enamored or trained in science, we can show interest and give encouragement in what he's learning and be enthusiastic about science fair projects at school. We can provide our child resources for activities and discoveries at home, such as the "Science by Mail" program (see below) or a nature kit, or remark, "Look at this front page article about the ozone layer!"

Following are some ways you can enrich your child's science learning:

- When your child has questions while studying his science homework, read aloud with him to help discover the answers. For questions about nature or something you don't know, look them up together or jot them down and pick up a book at the library later when you're doing errands. Your attitude of affirming questions and exploration goes a long way toward keeping an interest in science alive in your child.
- Teach your child to deal with failure constructively. In science projects and experiments, what children learn in the *process* is as important as the product. When an experiment or project doesn't work, share with your child, "It's okay, because scientists fail their way to success." We can point out that Edison failed hundreds of times in developing the light bulb and Salk failed countless times before finding a polio vaccine. Help your children be willing to tolerate moderate doses of failure and look at them as chances to say, "What can I learn from this? Now I know what doesn't work." Encourage them to stick with the project and take the risk of trying again (and again) and in the process gain some valuable perseverance.
- Subscribe to "Science-By-Mail," a program of the Boston

Museum of Science for fourth- through ninth-graders that sends science projects and materials to subscribers three times during the school year.[1]

- Make a birdhouse or bird feeder for the backyard with your child and fill it with sunflower seeds. Read a book about different species of birds and try to identify the birds that come to your feeder. Let your child grow a small vegetable garden on a small plot of land in your backyard or care for a tree. Collect and press its leaves in wax paper each season.
- Get a star map from a local planetarium or science museum and take a stargazing walk. Identify stars, planets, constellations, and different phases of the moon.
- Take a nature walk in the woods and don't forget to bring a magnifying glass to get a close up look at a flower or bug. Our family took paper bags to collect different varieties of wild flowers, pinecones, rocks, and leaves.
- Take a trip to the science museum, local zoo, or park. Discuss the differences between types of species, such as the Indian and African elephant.
- Buy a butterfly garden kit (it comes with cocoons and equipment), a frog hatchery kit, or an ant farm.[2] Have your child catch and study butterflies, or raise frogs or ants. He can then record his observations of these insects and reptiles in a "Nature Notebook."
- Encourage your child to collect shells, rocks, leaves, or stamps. Set aside a shoe box or shelf for the collection. He can learn valuable science classifying and categorizing skills.
- Watch nature and science television specials on public television channels.

- Purchase nature books for your family's library or check out science books at the public library. Many beautifully illustrated books are available on spiders or snakes, how leaves change, how machines work, and any topic you can imagine.
- Subscribe to a science magazine for your child, such as *Ranger Rick, National Geographic World, Super Science*, or *1-2-3 Contact*.
- Acquaint your child with the interesting lives of scientists, such as Thomas Edison, Louis Pasteur, and Marie Curie, by having him read their biographies. When you read *Surely You're Joking, Mr. Feynman,*[3] for instance, your child and might learn a lot of things a scientist was interested in as a child and perhaps identify with him and think, *Maybe I'll grow up to be a scientist.*
- Experiment with kitchen science. Let your child grow alfalfa sprouts or radishes. Put yeast on a banana and investigate the decomposition of food. Make bread and let him knead the dough. Talk about the growth of the yeast that makes the bread rise.
- Boil a fish and study its bone structure if your child is studying anatomy in school, or dissect the heart of a chicken and identify its chambers and ventricles. Dissect a flower or mushroom and identify its parts.
- Look for science articles in newspapers and magazines. Watch for television reports on medical or environmental updates.
- Brainstorm ideas for your child's science fair by looking through encyclopedias or going to science museums. Be sure your student starts his project far ahead of the deadline. The first thing he should do is make a list of the

supplies he will need. Then he needs to create a timetable for tasks to be done. Give him plenty of encouragement and support, but let the science fair project be *his*.

- Give him an illustrated or full-color book related to a science interest he has, such as astronomy, African animals, or chemical reactions.
- If there are several interested students, help start a science, engineering, or chemistry club at school. A science teacher can be a sponsor, and parents can help organize outings, such as a geology field trip or day at a local university science department.

HELPING YOUR CHILD WITH MATH

Math matters! During his elementary years your child will develop confidence and skill in math *or* decide that math is not for him. The everyday world around us is full of math, and whether you loved or hated it when you were in school, you can build your child's skills, interest, and confidence with some of the activities that follow and with your approach to math homework. Helping your child with math homework can be a challenge and takes lots of patience, but it reaps rich rewards. Here are some ways to help:

- Know what math skills are to be mastered at each grade level. For example, addition and subtraction are taught in the first and second grades; multiplication tables and division in the third and fourth grades; fractions in the fourth and fifth grades. (It is critical that your child master these basics or he'll be handicapped in figuring percentages, square roots, and more complicated algebraic calculations.)

Whether or not the teacher stresses memorization, make sure your child knows these computation skills like the back of his hand and doesn't have to rely on a calculator. Students should use calculators only after they understand the functions being performed and can do them by hand if asked.

- Teach kinesthetically inclined children (or kinesthetic learners) using active methods, such as counting while clapping, marching, or dribbling a basketball. Movement combined with oral drills helps the concepts "click."
- Show your child how to make his numbers line up in the appropriate columns when adding, subtracting, multiplying, or dividing.
- If your child is doing math homework and doesn't understand how to do a problem, have him first explain what he understands and has done. Instead of giving him the answer, walk him through each step of the problem by asking questions, such as, "What do you think we should try first? Now, what do we do next?" Make sure your child *understands* the reasons for the steps as he works the problem.
- Try various approaches to solving a problem. Draw pictures or use objects such as beans or blocks to illustrate mathematical processes. Straws can be used to illustrate fractions. Get a box of plastic straws in different colors. Cut all the red ones into fourths, the yellow straws in half, and the green ones into thirds.
- When middle school children need to study for a math test, encourage them to rework problems from past homework assignments and tests. If they have trouble, make sure they get help from the teacher well *before* the test.

- From middle school through high school, encourage your child to practice *estimating* skills. Shopping is a good place to practice estimating, using decimals and fractions. If your daughter wants to buy new socks, earrings, and a new blouse, encourage her to round off each price to the nearest $5.00 and mentally add the items together to see if she has enough allowance saved up for the needed purchases.
- Let your child apply mathematics skills to everyday needs. For example, if you need to order new carpet for a room, have him figure the square footage of the floor space and advise how much carpet you need to purchase. Or when you are planning a trip, have him call the hotel or campgrounds to determine nightly rates.
- Play "Mental Math" when you're riding in the car together or waiting at the doctor's office. First, start with an easy set of numbers, such as 2 + 4 x 3. Then add division: 2 + 4 x 3 ÷ 6.
- Help your middle school student set up a budget. He can use a small bookkeeping notebook and develop categories, such as tithe, savings, school lunches, and spending money. As a child gets older, he can manage his own clothing allowance.
- Let your child make a grocery list for his favorite meal and use newspaper ads to calculate the cost of the ingredients. Go shopping and see how close he was!
- Have your child clip and redeem coupons. My friend offered her eight-year-old son half of the savings from coupons he clipped and used. This has been a great help to her and a good source of extra money and math practice for him.
- Let your child keep a record of gas fill-ups using the following equation: total miles driven divided by number

of gallons purchased equals miles per gallon the car is getting.

- Give your child a mileage guide, map, and magic marker. Let him follow the route and check how far you've gone. Use a map to calculate the mileage to a friend's house. Estimate the distance between towns. Count barns, service stations, or VW Bugs along the highway.
- Play card games, such as hearts, spades, crazy 8s, go fish, and war to provide math practice and build skills, such as sorting, grouping, logic, and problem solving. Play family board games that require logic and math skills, such as Monopoly, Pay Day, chess, and checkers.
- If your child loves sports, have him keep up with sports page statistics or figure the baseball batting average of a favorite player using times at bat and number of hits: number of hits÷number of times at bat. For example, if a player comes up to bat five times and gets two hits, his batting average for that game is .400. This helps him see how useful math skills are in everyday life.
- Let your child help you make something from a recipe (older children can be responsible for cooking a whole meal). Following a recipe gives practice using fractions and working with measurements, time, and temperature. Help your child make the necessary calculations to double a cookie recipe. Then let him measure the ingredients and bake the cookies.
- Count trees on a walk, toys in a room, or days on a calendar with your child. Use number books, nursery rhymes, fairy tales, jumping-rope with rhymes, jacks, and hopscotch to teach a young child how to count.

- Sort laundry into lights and darks, set the table, put silverware away in the right places, or sort coins.
- Teach your child how to manage an allowance and save money. Help him set up a lemonade stand or include him in a family garage sale and let him price his clothing and toys.

HELPING YOUR CHILD WITH GEOGRAPHY

Why help your child learn geography? If he masters geography, he will have a *much greater chance* of enjoying and succeeding in American and world history. Students need to know what is where and be familiar with using maps and atlases. They need to understand direction, latitude, and longitude, know how to find locations, and appreciate the relationship between people and the places where they live.

Encourage your child's school to include several years of geography at both the elementary and secondary levels, and incorporate some of the following activities at home to enrich and increase his knowledge of geography:

- Get a good atlas for your home library and refer to it when questions come up about a state or another country.
- Use games to learn geography, such as "Games of the States," "Where in the World?" and "World Traveler." There are also great computer games and software, such as "PC Globe" for learning geography.
- Provide puzzles: Putting together puzzles of the United States and the world is a good way for a child to become familiar with where states and countries are located, especially kids with tactile and kinesthetic strengths.
- Get a map of your city and pick out familiar streets and

landmarks. Help your child find your street and mark it in yellow highlighter. Find the downtown area, lakes, rivers, parks, or places your child likes to visit.

- Using large butcher paper and markers, your child can make a map of his own neighborhood with your house, neighbors' and best friends' homes, landmarks, and buildings nearby. Help him learn to write down directions on how to get to school from your house or from your house to Grandma's house.
- Before taking a trip, look at a map of your route and destination with your child. Let your child hold a map and keep track of your trip in the car.
- Keep a world map or globe close to the television so you can point out places in the news or sports.
- Put a large U.S. map where the whole family can refer to it. Tack small pictures of friends and family near the cities where they live. If you go on a business trip, plot your route with colored string on the map. Laminated maps are handy because you can write on them with a grease pencil and wipe with a paper towel.
- When your child is learning states and capitals or other geographical facts at school, have him make flash cards with colored index cards (state on the front, capital on the back; or shape on the front, capital on the back; or shape on the front, name on the back) and practice saying them with a friend or member of the family.
- Play the license plate game when traveling with children to teach them the location of the states. Duplicate copies of a 8 1/2 x 11-inch U.S. map and give one to each child. When she sees a car from California, for example, she

finds the state on the map and fills it in—and on through as many states as possible. The person who fills in the most states by the end of the trip wins.

- Play "What state am I?"—another good game to play while you travel or do errands in the car. Each player takes a turn being a state. The first player gives a clue, such as "I am called the Lone Star State." If no one guesses it correctly, he gives a second or third clue before revealing the state. "I am the state that remembers the Alamo." "I am the state where John Kennedy was assassinated."

  Other examples might include: "I am the state known for my (Idaho) potatoes." "I am the state with the big oil (Alaska) pipeline." "I am the state farthest north on the eastern coast" (Maine). Keep a paperback atlas or almanac in the car so younger kids can look for their clues.
- Play "Name that state." This is a family game that builds memory skills. One player numbers from one to 50 on a piece of paper. The family names all the states they can remember and the player with the pencil and paper writes them down. After the group has named all the states they can remember, the recorder checks a map or atlas to see what states were left out.
- One night each week, serve food from a different country. Find the country on a map and read about it in an encyclopedia or book.
- Invite foreign-exchange students to dinner. Encourage them to bring pictures or maps of their country and to talk about their home life and customs. Ask them to teach you a song or greeting in their language.
- Check out books about people from foreign countries.

EARTH SAVERS

Here are some ideas to help your child enjoy the world of science and to help save our environment.

Plant a tree.[4] Trees remove large amounts of carbon dioxide from the atmosphere, thus fighting the greenhouse effect. Call or visit a local nursery to select a tree best suited for your locale. As a family, neighborhood, or school project, collect aluminum cans and recycle[5] to raise money for a bigger tree (as opposed to seedlings). Trees need care the first two years, so "adopt" the tree (provide water, staking, and mulch) and watch it grow!

Save our oceans and marine life. When you go to the beach, bring along a trash bag and spend a few minutes picking up beach litter—especially plastic bottles, cans, and six-pack rings. Since plastic waste kills up to a million seabirds and over 100,000 mammals and fish each year, taking the plastic off the beach saves lives![6] (Before you toss six-pack rings into the garbage, *snip each circle with blunt scissors;* they are especially dangerous to birds and marine life.)

Save our streams. Wherever you go—hiking, camping, or in state or community parks—removing trash out of streams is also very important. Picking up cans and litter helps clear the stream so water can flow and oxygen levels can return to normal, making it possible for fish and aquatic life to return.

Create a backyard wildlife habitat. You can make up for the loss of natural habitat by building a backyard refuge. A bird feeder on your fence or even on a city balcony can provide much-needed food for many species of birds; a bird bath provides water. Colorful flowers attract butterflies; red morning glories attract hummingbirds; fences and shrubs provide shelter for squirrels.

The National Federation of Wildlife suggests sketching out your yard and where you plan to plant, provide water, and shelter.

Then send your plan with $5.00 to the National Wildlife Federation Backyard Wildlife Habitat Program, 1412 16th Street N.W., Washington, D.C. 20036-2266. They will make suggestions and certify your yard as an official "Backyard Wildlife Habitat"—a great way to involve kids.

HELPING YOUR CHILD WITH HISTORY AND SOCIAL STUDIES

History, the story of what has happened in the life of a people or country, can be one of the most fascinating subjects your child learns. Unfortunately, the majority of history instruction in school is a textbook approach: Read these pages and take a test on Friday over the materials . . . memorize dates and definitions and get ready for the standardized test.

Recent research shows that many American students don't know the history of their country or even of their own family. One of the best things we as parents can do to reverse this trend is to help bring the study of history alive. Here are some ways to do this.

- Be a storytelling family! At the dinner table each evening, tell stories from every family member's day at school, work, or play. Also, sharing tales of your own school days, courtship, and life journey with your children gives them a sense of heritage and continuity *and* boosts their motivation for learning history.
- Help your child get the "big picture" of the year's social studies or history lessons. At the start of the school year, preview the textbook with him. Scan over the whole book; read the table of contents. Then you can plan ahead on ways to enrich his studies in class.
- From the beginning, help your child make a time line of

the historical period he is studying. A time line is invaluable for understanding the chronology of a period and developing a visual image of how events relate to each other and to large themes. Your child can add to the time line as the semester progresses. Use white butcher paper and bright markers and hang it on the wall around his room.

Your child can add a symbol or picture under each date and event that will greatly aid his remembering the dates and happenings. Here's an example:

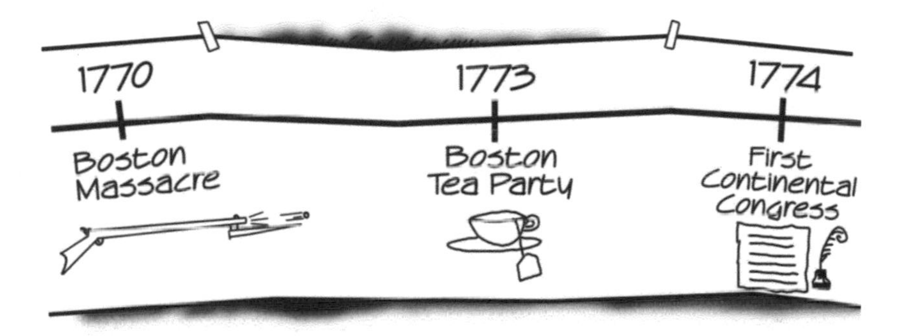

- Encourage your child to give attention to graphs, tables, and diagrams, which can clarify the relationship between ideas and events in history.
- Experience what it was like to live in a different era by visiting one of the many historical sites called "Living History Museums" in a state you travel to or in your area. You and your children can see what a restored, working 1880s farm is like, see a reenactment of revolutionary militia drills, or experience being a passenger on the *Mayflower*. Check with your state tourist bureau (or in the

area you'll be visiting) to see what living history museums are available to make history come alive.

- Have your child read a biography or novel (or even better, make it part of your family reading time) that corresponds to the era in history being studied. Reading the story of Robert E. Lee can enliven the study of the Civil War, for example. There are wonderful biographies of presidents, women pioneers, and heroes of each time in history, which you can check out of the library. Search for gems of information that show how real people lived during a historical period.
- Provide a cassette tape player for your child so she can tape record her own personal experience stories, pretend to be an on-the-scene reporter and narrate an event from the American Revolution, or practice speeches or oral reports for school.
- Check your local library and video store for videotape programs and documentaries on the eras they study that you can watch and discuss as a family.
- Help your child use memory techniques and learning style strategies to memorize facts and dates when necessary in history and social studies (see chapter 9 for suggestions).
- Whenever possible, have your child interview people in your extended family or neighborhood who have lived through a certain time or event in history he's studying at school. Help him prepare questions before the interview. Tape record and follow up with a written story or an oral sharing at the family dinner table of what he has learned.
- Encourage your child to look up answers to his questions in dictionaries, encyclopedias, and almanacs. It's helpful to

add these resources to your home library or check the reference section at your local library.

- When your child has a report to prepare for social studies or history class, go to the library together:
  1. Help him clarify what he's expected to do.
  2. Suggest he look up his topic in the card catalog and enlist the librarian's help in locating materials.
  3. Help him break the report into logical parts and have a step-by-step plan for completing each part of the project.
  4. Show interest, encourage, and brainstorm with your child, but avoid the temptation to take over the assignment and write it yourself.
  5. If your child enjoys art, encourage him to illustrate or make a poster to go with his report.
  6. A little review each day is better than cramming right before the history test, especially when there's a big volume of material. Several days to a week in advance, skim the textbook, listing the major ideas in the chapter. Next to each major idea, write the names, places, and dates of events that are most important. To review, you can name the main idea or concept and have your child say as many dates, people, and places he can remember that connect with it. Encourage critical thinking by discussing the why's, causes, and effects of events. How did one event cause another? What were the turning points in the historical period?
- Stamp collecting is a great way to stimulate a child's interest in history. Bill Mattox's grandfather worked for the post office when Bill was growing up and helped him develop a

big stamp collection. "My brothers and I learned more about significant political, social, and military events from collecting stamps than we ever did in the classroom," said Bill. "Here was something tangible: We got the new Nathan Hale stamp and wanted to look him up in a book and find out who he was and why a stamp was devoted to him." Collecting old coins, memorabilia, and even baseball cards can stir up a child's interest in history.

- Gary Bauer of the Family Research Council suggests that whether the founding documents of our democracy are taught in your child's school or not, *introduce them to your children*. Read them the Declaration of Independence, Washington's Farewell Address, Lincoln's Gettysburg Address, Martin Luther King's "I Have a Dream" speech, and other documents foundational to the heritage of America.[7]

By implementing some of these ideas, subjects such as science, math, geography, and history can come alive for your child. You can improve your child's performance in these areas during their academic years and beyond.

In the next chapter, we'll look at *spiritual* enrichment and how to build foundations at home that equip your child to grow strong in his values and beliefs while attending public schools.

CHAPTER 12

Implementing Character Education in Your Child's School

To educate a person in mind and not in morals
is to educate a menace to society.
—Theodore Roosevelt

Perhaps you're working to impart good values and solid character to your children at home. But what's happening at school, and what's being taught there?

One of the hopeful trends in public schools is the effort to turn from the values-free, do-whatever-feels-good philosophy of the past few decades to teaching good character and moral values. The trend is also directed at stemming the tide of violence that results when kids grow up in a moral vacuum, devoid of a sense of right and wrong. While parents and educators have been stunned by tragedies in our schools and the moral decline of both young and old, the concern for character and restoring moral values has grown. This concern has led communities and school districts across America to realize we can't just teach academics without helping to provide children with moral and ethical foundations.

As a parent, former teacher, and chairman of the county school board in Raleigh, North Carolina, Judy Hoffman was deeply concerned about the guns, fights, drugs, and disrespect she was seeing in the public schools. The year 83 weapons were found in students' possession, she knew something had to change.

A violence task force was formed, and after much deliberation, it brought recommendations that included metal detectors, more police officers on campus, clear book bags, and drug searches. But Judy knew those solutions alone wouldn't get to the root of why students were acting in destructive ways. She had heard of Ohio and Minnesota schools that were having great results with teaching values. After attending the annual Association of School Administrators conference in Orlando, Florida, and looking at examples of where character education was working, she came back to Wake County with a vision for how to put virtue and values back into public education.

With direction from the school board, Judy put together a 32-member task force that included people from different religions, races, neighborhoods, and professions. Made up of parents and business, religious, and community leaders, the task force identified core character traits acceptable to the community: respect, courage, integrity, self-discipline, kindness, responsibility, perseverance, and good judgment. And after Judy prayed for months about how to implement character education, along with much careful planning, the public schools in Wake County began a character education program.

Their program doesn't just have students completing a few workbook pages a week. Rather, virtue and character principles are integrated into lessons, literature, classroom rules, songs, plays, and teachable moments during instruction. Character is integrated into every area of the school day at all levels for the 90,000 students in the district.

The program is now more than five years old, and the results are impressive in both the education and behavior of students. There's a better academic climate, with teachers feeling more respected and able to really teach instead of just be on disciplinary duty. Test scores have gone up significantly at all grade levels. There's been a decrease in pregnancy rates and dropouts. And most importantly, violence, disturbances, and weapons seizures have all dropped significantly. In a better overall school environment, students feel safer and more respected.

Judy and her colleagues at Character Development Group in Raleigh, North Carolina, now consult with other schools and districts who want to develop character education programs, and she advises careful planning. "If you don't take the time to plan character education well, it can backfire," she says. "You must bring everyone to the table with your task force." She also developed a workbook titled *Character Education Workbook: A How-To Manual* that takes a school board or community leaders through a process to create an effective character education program.

Judy recommends a community or district develop its own curriculum with its parents, teachers, and church and business leaders instead of using a packaged program, because then you don't have to worry about something being there that you don't want taught to your students. You can choose the most important values you want to impart to the children of your community.

Since character education has been publicly endorsed by U.S. Secretary of Education Richard Riley and the majority of states are looking at how to teach character, it's a great time for Christian parents and educators to be involved. "We have a tremendous opportunity to affect people in our schools with the love of Christ and get in there and have a say about what our children are going to be taught and how to do it," says Judy. In order to do that, she advises:

- Be available to see how and where God wants to use you and how you can help.
- Be willing to serve in love and not judgment.
- Look for ways to help improve education for all children, not just your own.

Here are Judy's character education "Top 10" suggestions for schools:

1. *Model* the traits you want your students to exhibit.
2. *Affirm* the practice of good character with specific words and actions.
3. *Integrate* character education into all areas of the curriculum.
    - Identify where it already exists
    - Determine new character connections
    - Utilize the teachable moment
4. *Permeate* the school climate with the elements of character.
5. *Include* every member of the school community in the character education initiative.
6. *Enlist* the home and community at large as active partners in the process of character development.
7. *Involve* the students in designing your program and in planning character-related activities.

8. *Emphasize* the application of character traits in life situations, and teach decision-making skills.
9. *Establish* a character education team to lead the charge.
10. *Develop* resources—speakers, videos, quotes, and books—that focus on elements of character.

While the primary responsibility for developing the character of children lies with the family and church, schools can play an important role in teaching and reinforcing virtue. That's why any program in character education in public schools needs to draw heavily from the input of parents and the religious community.[1]

"Ultimately, character education, instilled by parents and the church and properly reinforced in the public school, can lead children to comprehend vital truths," say Perry Glanzer, Education Policy Analyst at Focus on the Family. "The best end of character education is not only the attainment of good character traits, but a recognition of the Source of virtue, a realization that one falls short of the standards that the Source sets, and the need for grace and mercy from that Source to attain true virtue."[2]

Character education is widespread and growing in the country. As of the time of this writing, 33 states had applied for federal grants from the U.S. Department of Education's "Partnerships in Character Education Pilot Project," and 21 had already received the grants. Early surveys from Character Education Partnership in Washington, D.C., show that at least 40 out of 50 states have either implemented character education or are developing programs. And it's not just federal funding that's supporting the initiatives; support is coming from all kinds of directions—from the business community, private foundations, local Chambers of Commerce, and school districts. As in the case of Wake County, North Carolina, an individual concerned about the need for character education (either an educator, parent, the governor, or business leader) spearheads local efforts.

Here are some organizations that promote character education by providing teacher training, classroom resources for character education, materials to help a community or school district shape its own character education program, or all three:

Center for the Advancement of Ethics and Character. 605 Commonwealth Avenue, Boston University, Boston, MA 02215. Ph: (617) 353-3262. The Center produces *Character*, a quarterly newsletter of the Association of Supervision and Curriculum Development's Character Education Network. In addition, it provides *100 Ways to Promote Character Education*, a list of suggestions compiled by staff at the center. Contact: Dr. Kevin Ryan.

Center for the 4th and the 5th R's. Education Department, State University College at Cortland, P.O. Box 2000, Cortland, NY 13045. Ph: (607) 753-2455. Fax: (607) 753-5980. Contact: Dr. Thomas Lickona. Web site: http://www.cortland.edu/www/c4n5rs/index.html.

Character Development Foundation. P.O. Box 4782, Manchester, NH 03108-4782. Ph: (603) 472-3063. The Foundation provides teacher training for public-school teachers. Contact: Dr. Lori Wiley.

Character Education Institute. 250 University Ave., California (city), PA 15419. Ph: (412) 938-4500. Fax: (412) 938-4156. Contact: Dr. Henry Huffman.

Character Education Partnership. Ph: (800) 988-8081. The Partnership is a clearinghouse for information about character education programs used in public schools. Web site: www.character.org.

Character Development Group. P.O. Box 9211, Chapel Hill, NC 27515-211. Ph: (919) 967-2110. Fax: (919) 967-2139. Contact: Dr. Phil Vincent, Dickson Smith, Judy Hoffman.

Children of the World/North American School Project. 910 Calle Negocio, Suite 300, San Clemente, CA 92673-6521. Ph: (714) 361-4591. This division of Campus Crusade for Christ has developed a character education curriculum, along with a teacher education program, that can be used in public and private Christian schools. Contact: Vernie Schorr; Web site: http://www.character.com.

The Council for Religion in Independent Schools. 4405 East West Highway, #401, Bethesda, MD 20814-4535. Ph: (301) 657-0912. Fax: (301) 657-0915.

Critical Thinking Press & Software. P.O. Box 448, Dept. 4, Pacific Grove, CA 93950-0448. Ph: (800) 458-4849. Fax: (408) 393-3277. Publishes "Exploring Ethics Through Children's Literature," a literature-based ethics program for grades two through six.

Ethics Resource Center, Inc. 1120 G. Street, NW, Suite 200, Washington, D.C. 20005. Ph: (800) 777-1285.

Medical Institute for Sexual Health. P.O. Box 4919, Austin, TX 48765. Ph: (800) 892-9484. Publishes the *National Guidelines for Sexuality and Character Education*, whose aim is to help schools integrate abstinence-based sexuality education and character education. It also contains a helpful appendix of character- and abstinence-based sex-education resources.

PREP of St. Louis. 13157 Olive Spur Road, St. Louis, MO 63141. Ph: (800) 478-5684. Fax: (314) 576-4996. PREP has helped establish character-education programs in

22 public school districts in St. Louis.

The School for Ethical Education. 1000 Lafayette Blvd., Bridgeport, CT 06604. Ph: (203) 330-5052. Fax: (203) 330-5036. Contact: Dr. David Wangaard. The School provides teacher training for character education.

STARS (Students Taking a Right Stand). P.O. Box 8936, Chattanooga, TN 37411. Ph: (800) 477-8277. Fax: (615) 899-4547. STARS publishes character-education material and provides character-education training.

Wise Skills Resources. 1810 Hardison Place No. 10, South Pasadena, CA 91030. Ph: (818) 441-7944. Web site: http://www.cris.com/~Wskills.

CHARACTER-EDUCATION RESOURCES FROM FOCUS ON THE FAMILY

The following resources are available in both public-school and Christian versions. To order, please call: (800) 932-9123 or write: Focus on the Family Education Resources, P.O. Box 15379, Colorado Springs, CO 80935-5379.

Pre-K through 3rd Grade: "Adventures in Odyssey" Videos

Go West, Young Man

Teaches kids the importance of integrity and of keeping their word.

Shadow of a Doubt

Gives students an unforgettable lesson in loyalty, faithfulness, and friendship.

The Knight Travelers

Encourages kids to focus on priorities and what's truly important in life.

Once Upon an Avalanche
Highlights an inspirational example of kindness and brotherly love.

A Flight to the Finish
Promotes caring through a fast-paced cliffhanger.

Star Quest
Points out the difference between being selfish and being a friend.

A Fine Feathered Frenzy
Shows children the value of being responsible.

3rd through 6th Grade: "Last Chance Detectives" Videos
Escape from Fire Lake
While looking for clues, one of the detectives turns up missing. In the search for him, the characters all learn what perseverance really means.

Legend of the Desert Bigfoot
The young sleuths learn the importance of discernment and doing the right thing.

Mystery Lights of Navajo Mesa
The four budding investigators learn about friendship and forgiveness when they end up solving two cases at the same time.

3rd through 6th Grade: "McGee and Me" Videos
Skate Expectations
In this fast-paced skateboard adventure, Nicholas learns the value of being respectful to others no matter who they are.

Do the Bright Thing
On an imaginative tour through his brain, Nick learns about the

process and payoff of making right-and-wrong decisions.

The Not-So-Great Escape
Nick's parents won't let him see a movie that "everyone else" is going to see. But going anyway, he soon understands the value of obeying his mom and dad.

Take Me Out of the Ball Game
With the help of baseball great Orel Hershiser, kids learn the importance of good sportsmanship.

The Big Lie
With a little help, Nicholas discovers that telling lies is not the way to make friends.

The Blunder Years
When Nick stumbles into the popularity pitfall, he quickly learns that the right jeans, shirts, and shades are no match for a loving attitude and strong character.

Back to the Drawing Board
Nick and McGee both learn that jealousy causes hurt, anger, and frustration—especially to the one who's jealous.

7th through 12th Grade: Sex, Drugs, and Character Education

Molder of Dreams
In this video, Guy Doud, a former national teacher of the year, uses humor and warmth to show that we hold one another's fragile hopes in our hands, that everything we say and do has the potential to shape another's dreams, and that the most profound lessons you learn in school are the ones you learn about yourself.

Masquerade
A dramatic exposé featuring Milton Creagh that reveals the devastating consequences of drugs and alcohol.

No Apologies
A fast-paced video exposé on the risks of premarital sex.

No Apologies Curriculum
An abstinence-based curriculum to teach students good judgment, courage, fairness, and self-control.

Other Character Education Books and Resources
Available from Focus on the Family

Educating for Character
This book by Thomas Lickona is the seminal work in the field. It outlines a basic approach to character education and offers numerous examples of its application in schools.

Right from Wrong
A book by Josh McDowell and Bob Hostetler that discusses the declining state of morality among Christian youth and what can be done about it.

Other Resources
Books that Build Character
A helpful resource compiled by William Kilpatrick and Gregory and Suzanne M. Wolf.

The Book of Virtues
William Bennett's compilation of children's stories that extol and reinforce a variety of virtues such as self-discipline, compassion, responsibility, and faith.

National Guidelines for Sexuality and Character Education
These guidelines are designed by the Medical Institute for Sexual Health and one of the foremost character-education experts, Thomas Lickona. Their aim is to help schools achieve the integration of abstinence-based sexual education and character education. The guidelines also contain a helpful appendix of character- and abstinence-based sex-education resources. Published by Medical Institute for Sexual Health. Ph:(800) 892-9484.

Why Johnny Can't Tell Right from Wrong
William Kilpatrick argues that basic morality is not taught in our schools. In addition, he provides numerous suggestions for how parents and teachers can impart values to children.

With any of the above books, videos, programs, or approaches to character education, it's important to remember that only by involving the whole school, community, and parents will improvement happen not only in the behavior of students, but also in the core values they internalize. If you hold public meetings and give everyone—churches, PTAs, business people, educators, and parents—the opportunity to hear about character education *and* share in its development, a sense of ownership and cooperation can develop that will improve children's lives and futures.

CHAPTER 13

Helping Your Child Strengthen His Faith

Matt, a Kansas middle school student, started playing basketball competitively in the fourth grade. He had played "Horse" with his dad on the driveway for many years, but at 10 he was ready to join a team. His community practically worshipped the sport, and to be recognized by the local basketball coaches, a player had to begin early. Matt gave 110 percent at every practice, lifted weights in the mornings before school, and played basketball with his dad in the evenings.

Although he made a lot of progress and was well respected by his coaches and teammates, Matt was not chosen for the traveling team that would go to the national tournaments. Instead, he found his name on the list of mediocre players. Because he was dedicated to the sport, Matt decided to play for the team anyway.

However, he continued to dream of playing for the traveling team.

After his eighth-grade year, Matt learned that the traveling team had been invited to compete in the national tournament in Florida. A few days later, the coach called him and invited him to play with the team in Florida. Matthew was elated. Finally his hard work was paying off. However, there was one catch—since Matt was one month too old to be eligible for the tournament, he would have to lie about his age.

"It's very common for players to change their ages. No one ever finds out," his coach told him. "Besides, a good performance in this competition can give you the edge you need to play on the varsity team at school." Matt felt sick. He had never wanted anything more than to play on the traveling team, but he knew that lying about his age would be wrong. Matt discussed the situation with his parents, who encouraged him to consider the consequences but left the decision up to him. "We want to let you work through this one yourself," they said.

Despite Matt's strong desire to play on the team, he knew the decision he had to make. He said no.

What enabled Matt to do what he knew was right? Why was he faithful to the values his family had taught him? How can a child be prepared at home to stand strong in Christ no matter what the cost?

LOVING YOUR CHILD

To stand alone for their beliefs, children need to know that they are loved unconditionally and supported at home. Parents need to teach their children that their self-worth comes from God. At a young age, children can learn that they are valuable to God and made in His image. If a child's self-worth is based on an unchanging foundation, he will not be as susceptible to peer pressure.

SPENDING TIME WITH YOUR CHILD

Bill Mattox, Jr., a policy analyst with the Family Research Council, observed:

> Contrary to the claims of professional children's advocates in Washington, the number one problem facing American children today is not lack of subsidized day care centers, or poor nutrition, or declining school performance. Nor is it poverty, though 20 percent of our children live below the poverty line.
>
> American children face a crisis of another kind—one that rivals our budget and trade problems: a deficit of time spent with their parents.[1]

Despite the hectic pace of life and the demands of school, work, extracurricular activities, and church commitments, the parents I interviewed say time with their kids is a top priority. These parents make sacrifices to be available to their kids. Moms give up their careers to have time to read to their children, play with them, take them to the park, or listen to them when they come home from school. Some single, working moms join their child for lunch if the school is nearby. Dads spend time with their children in the evenings. They help with projects, attend sports activities, and have devotions with them. Some working parents sacrifice a vacation day to chaperone their child's field trip or outing.

During times together with their children, parents can take

advantage of "teachable moments" to share their values with their children. One mom learned that even an activity as simple as baking cookies provides an opportunity to pass along values. As she got out the different ingredients for the recipe, she remarked on how bitter or sour some of them tasted by themselves, but how wonderful they tasted after being mixed together. "This makes me think of how God brings different circumstances into our lives. Some of them are pleasant while others are difficult, but they all work together for God's glory and our good," she told her daughter.

Even being the family taxi driver offers opportunities for parents to grow closer to their kids. Joe White of Kanakuk-Kanakomo Kamps advises parents who drive kids to soccer, piano, gymnastics, and school, "Make the taxi ride the greatest time in the world, make it party time, make it memory time."

TEACHING YOUR CHILD TO STAND ALONE

"I'm concerned that many children from Christian families do not know how to take a stand for what is right," said Jeff Myers of Summit Ministries. "What would happen if parents told their children 'Take a stand for what you believe, even if that stand displeases your teachers, and know that I will stand behind you'?"[2]

Jack and Susan Dabney's nine children went through the public schools in West Virginia and Virginia. They felt one of the most helpful things they did for their children was to teach them that it's okay to be different.

Standing up for what is right is not easy. Jay Abramson said, "We've prayed that God would help our children identify truth and have the courage to stand up for what they know is right."

Bill Mattox said he tried to teach his daughter Allison that the world has different values than God's values. For example, he encouraged her to love everyone, not just the popular kids in her class. He tried to teach her to reach out to her classmates who seemed lonely or who didn't fit in with the other kids. Remembering her father's words, Allison noticed a handicapped classmate who didn't know anyone at school, and she invited her to lunch. Allison continued to befriend the girl and invited her to come home with her. There, the girl told Allison that she had thought she would never have a friend at school and that Allison was the best friend she'd ever had. Sometimes, however, kids don't receive the kindness of our children with open arms as this child did. That's why we must also teach our kids how to handle the hurt they'll experience if they reach out to new students and then get dumped.

READING THE BIBLE AS A FAMILY

"The most important thing Debbie Jo and I have ever done as parents of these four kids of ours is memorizing Scripture with them," said Joe White. "The verses have turned into chapters and the chapters have turned into books."

Roxanne Pierce, a Maine mother, said, "We read the Bible with our kids in the morning before school. Our children also learn scriptures at church which we practice at home. Our daughter Sarah has a file box in which she stores all the verses she has memorized. God's Word is our absolute, and when we have family conflicts or disagreements we look to the Bible."

Many parents read Bible stories to their children after dinner or at bedtime. This is an example to them of the importance of spending time with the Lord and His Word every day. Devotionals, such as *Little Visits With God*, *Keys for Kids*, and *Family Walk*, work well.

Families need to be flexible with their devotional time. Jay Abramson understands the struggle of finding time to have family devotions. "With four boys in grade, middle, and high school, it isn't easy to do devotions. It's crazy in the mornings with school starting at different times, so we aim now for having family devotions after the evening meal." When the boys were younger, Jay read Bible stories from a picture book, but now they read a psalm and a New or Old Testament story. Then they spend some time praying together about tests, friends, or problems.

Jay meets with his older boys for breakfast on Saturdays to discuss their faith. In a year's time, they will read through the Old Testament, focusing on important historical and doctrinal passages. The following year they will read through the New Testament. They select key verses from their study to memorize as well. "It's like a Rubik's cube, like many squares of color," says Jay. "Kids get a Bible fact at Sunday school and pick up a spiritual concept at another place, but they may not know how they fit together; they may be all mixed up. The purpose of our time together will be to bring all the pieces together in one place, and help them see the covenant relationship of God with His people throughout the Bible."

If your children's ages vary greatly or if they are at different maturity levels, you can have individual devotional times. Fern Nichols says she had one devotional time with her two older boys and a second one with her two younger children.

It is also important to help our children develop their own personal time with God. Jay works with his older boys to provide resources and share what he does during his own quiet time. He has told them, "God wants a relationship with you and here's how you can start."

Gayla Morsman, an Edmond, Oklahoma, mom, says, "I've always told our children that they can talk to us or God about their problems." Her 15-year-old daughter Elizabeth has her own quiet time before bed.

When riding in the car to school, sitting around the table, or even jumping on the trampoline, Judy Hartsock centers her dialogue with her sons on biblical values. In every circumstance, her family tries to look to God's Word for wisdom. At bedtime they read devotional material, such as *Real Heroes Eat Hamburgers* or Michael W. Smith's book *Old Enough to Know*. Make time with God and His Word a priority so your children can grow in their knowledge of God and discern different philosophies and values at school.

"God asks us to be faithful to do our part in loving our children unconditionally, teaching them the Word of God, and taking them to church," says Fern Nichols. "As a mom I've had to learn how to leave the impossible parts to God—I can't change their heart or give them right thinking or make them love Jesus. That's the Holy Spirit's part."

MODELING A CHRISTIAN LIFESTYLE FOR YOUR CHILD

Children learn by watching and imitating. The model parents provide has a powerful impact in transferring values. "Our children see us studying the Bible on a daily basis and being active in church," says Carl Rehberg, an instructor at the Air Force Academy in Colorado Springs, Colorado.

"Living what we teach and being consistent is important to us as parents," says Roxanne Pierce. "When we make mistakes with our kids, we apologize to them. We try to be imitators of God and to walk in love."

"Modeling honesty and integrity, a love for God and for others, and biblical servanthood has had a big impact on our children's lives. Besides serving at their school, we do a lot of community work, because we want our children to know how important it is to care for others," says Kris Olsen, a Waco, Texas, mother.

Families can serve the community by distributing Meals-on-Wheels to shut-ins, gathering clothing and food for homeless people, collecting baby items for a crisis pregnancy center, or doing yard work for the elderly. These family activities can be followed by a fun activity, such as going out for pizza. A family could also sponsor a child through Compassion International or another missionary agency and raise the support money each month.[3]

MAINTAINING COMMUNICATION

One of the biggest challenges we face when guiding children through the turbulent waters of adolescence is keeping communication open. We need to be careful not to overreact when they question Christian beliefs. We can drive them away from Christianity if we stifle their questions with a legalistic or condemning response. Help your young people think through the issues, discuss them together, allow for differences of opinion, and steer them to appropriate reading material and resources.

"We have found that our children have to make their choices and internalize their values at a young age," said Nancy Chapman, a Dallas, Texas, mother of two teenagers. "Russ and Jan both had to decide early which groups they wanted to be a part of." Jan was a cheerleader and her group was made up of social, partying girls. She had to decide which people she was going to be with and why. It wasn't enough to say, "Oh, I can't go drinking tonight because I'm busy." Jan had to state her values on the matter.

When Jan's friends started getting physically involved with their boyfriends, Nancy bought Joe White's *Looking for Love in All the Wrong Places* and Josh McDowell's book *Dating, Picking (and Being) a Winner*. They read them together and talked about how Jan could use the information to help her friends. "I tend to be very protective and conservative. We needed to read and talk about the issues and dilemmas she was facing," Nancy added.

Although Russ had always been very open and communicative, when he began listening to rock music during seventh grade, he withdrew from the family. He spent a lot more time alone in his room listening to it nonstop before and after school. The Chapmans grew concerned.

"I decided that we needed to discuss his behavior together," said Nancy. "So I bought books on rock music that gave profiles of rock musicians and groups. I encouraged him to read about the rock-and-roll subculture."

After reading about the lifestyles of his idols, Russ threw away his tapes and compact discs and began listening to Christian contemporary music. He has shared his faith with all of his friends through Christian music. Today Russ leads a band that witnesses for Christ in his high school.

DEALING WITH YOUR CHILD'S DOUBTS

One of the biggest challenges for parents is to help our junior high and high school students develop critical thinking skills. We need to keep an open dialogue with them about the issues and situations they face. "When children make a statement contrary to your values, reason with them instead of overreacting," says Wendy Flint, mother and former school board president in Vancouver, Washington. "Help them go through the thought processes. Our moral standards must be upheld in the home. But if we're so strict that our young people can't choose, if we do all their thinking, we may drive them away from our home and God."

One day after school, Wendy's son came home with the idea that we should all accept homosexuality. "I don't know why you think it's wrong," he said, explaining his views and what his teacher had said.

His mother encouraged him to think about what determines right and wrong. Then she asked him to think about how his teacher might respond to the same question. She asked him questions, such as, "What is the purpose of sex?" "If God created sex, what is it designed for?" "What does the Bible say about homosexuality?" "What are the societal, medical, emotional, and psychological implications of the homosexual lifestyle?" She wanted him to thoroughly understand the biblical argument for the immorality of homosexuality so that he would not be easily swayed to consider opposing views.

GIVING YOUR CHILD CHRISTIAN INSTRUCTION AT SCHOOL

The bell rings in a Utah high school and several students gather their books, walk down the hall, cross the school lawn, and enter a nearby seminary. They attend a 60-minute elective course titled "Christian Living Skills." At the end of the class period, they return to their high school for the rest of their courses.

What are these students doing? They are involved in Released Time Christian Education—an opportunity for Christian-based teaching during the public school day. It provides children and teenagers a supplement to their training at church and home and takes place off-campus.

Although the concept has been used since 1914, a Supreme Court decision in 1952 established the constitutionality of Released Time.[4] Released Time programs are currently active in over 22 states, with over 250,000 children involved nationwide. Every school district in Oregon has at least one Released Time program. One of the best-developed programs is in Ellijay, Georgia, where the Christian Living Center, a 4,000-square-foot building, sits beside the public high school buildings. With broad community support from all denominations, the Christian Living Center has two full-time teachers instructing six classes a day.

After offering the Released Time program for seven years, this school reports a decrease in teenage pregnancy, vandalism, and drug and alcohol use. There have been no suicides. Teen church attendance is up, and teachers say the atmosphere and behavior in the classroom is markedly improved.

Released Time Christian Education classes emphasize basic foundations of faith (rather than denominational or doctrinal issues) and teach skills for living, such as getting along with parents, dealing with peer pressure, and staying pure for marriage.[5]

Parents and churches can start a Released Time education program in their community by contacting the National Association for Released Time Christian Education, 5722 Lime Ave., Long Beach, CA 90805. Phone: (800) 360-7943.

PROVIDING SUPPORT FOR CHRISTIAN YOUNG PEOPLE

Christian young people need to have friends who share their values and beliefs. Participating in a weekly Bible study, a church youth group, or a Christian organization such as Student Venture or Fellowship of Christian Athletes (FCA) helps young people stay on track with their faith and resist peer pressure.

Through Student Venture, Lin Smith's children gained personal ministry skills, hosted evangelistic outreaches for their athletic teams, and participated in weekly Bible studies. Student Venture taught her daughter to share her faith and gave her opportunities to witness in Manila, Mexico City, and Moscow.

Most parents I interviewed felt that choosing a church with a strong youth program was vital. "Being active in a church youth group kept Jan and Russ from standing alone in their faith. It helped them feel braver," said Nancy Chapman. "When you're a teenager, even one other student who shares your values can give you a lot of courage."

Following are Christian groups that support and reach out to young people:

Fellowship of Christian Athletes (FCA): A non-denominational ministry active in many junior high, high school, and college campuses in all 50 states. Its focus is "to present to athletes and coaches, and all whom they influence, the challenge and adventure of receiving Jesus Christ as Savior and Lord, serving Him in their relationships and in the fellowship of the church."

Fellowship of Christian Athletes
8701 Leeds Road
Kansas City, MO 64129
(816) 921-0909

Young Life: A source of fellowship for Christian kids that reaches out to unchurched teenagers. Young Life provides Campaigner groups (small group Bible studies for both boys and girls), and summer and weekend camps. However, their ultimate goal is to help kids find a biblical church. The heartbeat of the ministry is building relationships between the high schoolers and the Christian adult leaders. "Wild Life" is Young Life's ministry to junior high students.

Young Life
P. O. Box 520
Colorado Springs, CO 80901
(719) 473-4262

Student Venture: A high school ministry of Campus Crusade for Christ. Student Venture consists of thousands of high school students and 500 full-time staff and volunteers. The leaders present the gospel to school and athletic groups. They also conduct weekly meetings, weekend retreats, and training conferences.

Student Venture
100 Sunport Lane
Orlando, FL 32809
(800) 789-5462

Youth for Christ: A ministry that communicates the life-changing message of Jesus Christ to young people. That mission is carried out through the "Campus Life" high school and junior high school ministries. Youth for Christ has inner-city programs, ministry opportunities through "Project Serve" in the U.S. and other countries, and recovery centers for adolescents addicted to drugs or alcohol.

Youth for Christ
P. O. Box 228822
Denver, CO 80222
(303) 843-9000

How can these organizations be started in a school or community? A parent usually asks a coach or teacher in his child's school to start a group. Several moms in Norman, Oklahoma, went to their middle school track coach and asked him if he would help get an FCA group started. The parents offered to help by holding meetings in their homes, finding speakers, and sponsoring activities.

Besides FCA, Sunday school, and youth group, Judy Hartsock's boys have attended a neighborhood Bible study since elementary school. She and another mom hosted the Bible study in their homes. Other parents in the neighborhood and school began to ask, "Can my child be in the weekly group?"

When the Curtis family moved to a small Michigan town several years ago, their seventh-grade daughter couldn't find a Christian friend her age. With her family, she planned an "evangelistic kidnap breakfast." After inviting them beforehand, they picked up several girls in Elizabeth's class. They ate breakfast, and then listened to a talk about self-image given by a Campus Crusade staff member. Elizabeth continued her friendships with these girls and over the last two years, *half* of them became Christians. This past fall, they asked Elizabeth to start and teach a Bible study for them. They went together to a Christian bookstore to select a study guide.

"We are beginning to see the fruit of our labors as our high schoolers become personally dependent on Christ in their own walk and able to positively influence the lives of their friends and classmates," says Carolyn Curtis. As her children continued to grow in Christ throughout their high school experience and college years, they led both prayer groups and Bible studies for their peers.

Following is a self-test that measures how well parents are

providing spiritual foundations for their child and indicates what areas need more focus:

- How much time do you spend with your child each day?
- What interests or hobbies do you and your child pursue together?
- What are the five values most important to you that you hope to convey to your child?
- What are you doing to instill these values in your child?
- How are you involved in your child's school?
- Does your child know you'll support him if he takes a stand for what he believes?
- Have you taught your child that it's okay to go against the crowd?
- How often do you have family devotions?
- Does your child spend time in prayer and studying the Bible?
- Does your child see you serving in the community, church, or school?
- Is your child involved in a Christian support group?

CHAPTER 14

Praying for Your Child

Prayer has a special place in our lives as we guide our children through their growing up and schooling years. Regardless of where our children go to school, we cannot put them in a protective bubble until they get entirely through adolescence (although sometimes we'd like to). We cannot be in the car with them after every football game or movie. We can't control *all* the forces that seem to undo our training and care.

Even Christian kids raised in the church go through difficult times that try their faith (and ours), get in with the wrong crowd, or even at times compromise their values. Christian young people sometimes push away from us as they journey through the separation process that they must inevitably go through to become independent adults and stand on their own two feet someday.

As our children grow and we gradually lose direct control, we have a vital, important resource to support them and cooperate with God's working in their lives—prayer.

Every parent I interviewed felt prayer was the anchor of their family's experience in public schools. Whether it was prayer about a specific textbook problem that had arisen or a child struggling with a reading problem, prayer was an integral part of their stories.

As Susan Stewart, an Oklahoma City mom, said, "I feel that prayer is the most important tool I have. If I didn't pray for Andrew I'd feel like I was throwing him out to the wolves—without any armor, weapons, or protection! God hasn't provided a way to put him in private school, so I have no other choice right now but the public junior high. I have concerns, but as I pray, I have peace that the Lord is going to watch over him."

At the beginning of Andrew's seventh-grade year, all the students from his junior high, along with kids from other junior highs, were scheduled to go to Camp Classen. They would be staying in cabins for three days and do outdoor science activities. "I was not real comfortable about his taking off with teachers, parents, and counselors I don't know," said Susan. "But this was a big school event; we had to let him go." She prayed before he went and while he was gone.

When Andrew got home on Friday, he said he'd had a great time. "But the best thing about the trip was my cabin counselor. He was a great guy! The boys started talking about sex, and our counselor asked, 'Do you think you should have sex before marriage?' The other boys said, 'Yeah, sure, I probably will,' and 'Okay, yeah, I would too.' But I said, 'No, not until marriage.' And my counselor said, 'Way to go, Brother!' "

Several days later they found out that his counselor was a junior high teacher and a committed Christian. "Thank you, Lord, for putting Andrew in a protected place and with a godly teacher. You were watching out for Andrew!" Susan said.

PRAYER: THE FOUNDATION OF INVOLVEMENT

When Wendy Flint enrolled the first of her three children in the Evergreen district of Vancouver, Washington, public schools, she was hesitant and even fearful. But as she prayed, she was reassured that God would be with her children. She was convinced there were two things He wanted her to do: pray for her children and their schools every day, and second, get involved and become a part of the schools.

Over the years of her children's schooling, Wendy volunteered in a total of 21 classrooms, served as PTA president, became president of the school board, and founded the American Parents Association, a national organization that empowers parents with training and resources to make a difference in their school boards and local schools. And it all started with *prayer.*

PRAYER MAKES A DIFFERENCE IN THE PRAY-ER

Prayer makes a difference, but often it *first* changes the attitudes and actions of the one praying. When our daughter Alison was in the third grade, she was assigned to a third/fourth combined class with a young first-year teacher. I soon realized that Alison wasn't bringing papers home regularly, and when she did bring home an occasional spelling test, some words were mismarked. I called to ask how Alison was doing, but the teacher was vague. I heard from other parents that classroom discipline was loose, and I realized that might be why Alison found it hard to concentrate.

At first I was frustrated and even angry. Why hadn't she been put in a more experienced teacher's class? But the more I prayed about the problem, the more I felt I needed to ask the teacher if she needed help. When I did offer to help one day a week grading papers and assisting small reading groups, her face showed tremendous relief. She shared how overwhelmed she felt with the two grades together, trying to meet all their different needs (and deal with several fourth-graders who were discipline problems). By my pitching in with grading and giving individual students extra help, the children got feedback on their work faster, and she got a handle on some of the discipline problems.

PRAYER MAKES A DIFFERENCE—IN YOUR KIDS, THEIR SCHOOLS, FRIENDS, AND FAMILIES

When ordinary parents pray, extraordinary things happen. Many parents told me how prayer made a difference in their children's lives, their schools, and friends. Roxanne and Daniel Pierce have prayed consistently for guidance concerning their daughter Sarah's education and feel God has led them to the public school in their community at this time. Besides praying for Sarah's teachers and classmates, they prayed often that their daughter would lead others to Christ and be a laborer for Him. This has been answered in a wonderful way. So far, starting at age four, in kindergarten, she has led six children to the Lord.

Charity started first grade in New Hampshire this year, and her mom, Marci, is already convinced of God's answers to prayer. "My husband and I prayed for a Christian friend for Charity," says Marci. "And the teacher placed another Christian girl who also rides on the same school bus right next to her in the classroom. They are best buddies now and we have gotten to know the family. I came to know Christ because my best friend in public school was a Christian. I don't know where I would be today if her parents had sent her to a private school 25 years ago!"

Joanie Cassity moved with her family to Coppell, Texas, and began praying with a few other mothers for the elementary school her children attended. Within two years, the town had grown so rapidly that another elementary school was being built, and she learned they would lose most of their faculty plus the principal to the new school. Quite concerned about the instability this could produce, Joanie doubled her prayers for God to bring just the new staff members that would be best for the school, people who would have godly values and continue the excellent programs for the children. By September, the school had 18 new teachers, all caring, committed Christians, a Christian principal and school counselor, and the year was off to a great start.

When ordinary parents pray, extraordinary things happen.

The Smith family purposed to share Christ with the people in their spheres of influence. As their children started school and began activities, such as soccer and scouts, they asked the Lord for one family they could reach out to—by praying for that family faithfully and regularly for a year and spending time with them. They often prayed that their lifestyle would reflect God's love so much that people would ask them, "What makes your family so different?" and thus give them the opportunity to share what Christ means to them. During those elementary years, they saw four families come to Christ and all the parents and children grow and become active in churches.

Here are some things I've learned from my own experience and from these parents about praying effectively for our children and schools.

PRAY SPECIFICALLY

After their evening meal as many nights as possible, the Abramson family has prayer together with their four boys. "We work hard at keeping prayers from being like a TV commercial, the same thing every day," says Jay. "So we talk about what we are going to pray for. Are there tests? Needs you have? People we feel a concern for? We walk it through, and then divvy up the needs and everyone prays for different things. And we always pray that God will help our boys discern what is true, deal with it honestly, and have the courage to stand up for it."

Rowell and Corrie Sargeant, an Oklahoma City couple, check with each of their four children regularly for things they are struggling with or want them to pray about—friends, a problem at school, or a test. And they let their children know they are praying daily for them according to Deuteronomy 28:13—that the Lord will make them "the head and not the tail," meaning they will be a *positive* influence.

"One thing I do each year, the day school is over and all summer, I set aside time to pray for the teachers my children will be assigned to the next year," says Carolyn Curtis. "I pray that they will be assigned the exact teacher or teachers that they need, and I pray for every subject and for their schedules."

You could pray specifically:

- for God's guidance concerning what school is best for your child
- for the selection of teachers and then regularly pray for the teachers your child has

- that your children will form friendships with those who will build up their faith.

WORSHIP GOD, FOCUSING ON HIM AND NOT THE PROBLEMS

"When you learn how to worship God, it gets your eyes refocused on Him instead of all the problems your child or the school may be having," says Diane Myers, a single mother of four boys in Washington state. "It puts our problems in the right perspective to worship God for who He is, what He is like, what He has done and will do for us."

"Those who *know* Thy name will put their trust in Thee. . . ." says Psalm 9:10. One of the joys of praying with other mothers the last two years has been that, along with thousands of other Moms in Touch groups, we begin with *praise*, focusing on a different attribute of God each week. One week I chose the attribute that He is the One who cares for me. Different moms read verses aloud, such as Isaiah 27:3, Psalm 23, Deuteronomy 11:10-15, and 1 Peter 5:7.

These prayer groups can help us focus on God during tough times. One mother shared briefly a time when she had treatment for breast cancer and felt especially cared for by God. We prayed together, either silently or orally, each praising God for His faithful care of us and our families. That week was especially difficult for me with writing deadlines, recovering from the flu, and getting ready to go out of town to give seminars at a teachers' convention. I was also concerned about our daughter and the stress she felt trying to balance sports and youth group activities at our church.

As we focused on God's loving care, I was able to let go of these burdens and put them in God's hands, trusting that He cared greatly and could handle our problems! Later, a mom in our group shared that she had a difficult situation at work that week that needed God's care. She said she was strengthened and encouraged to trust Him more with this problem because of our prayer time.

For every need, problem, or trial we *or* our children have, there is something about God's character and presence that can see us through triumphantly.

LET SCRIPTURE GUIDE YOUR PRAYERS

Daily Bible reading and study is a great help in praying effectively for our children. Jean Fleming, in *A Mother's Heart*, suggests that we look for character qualities as we read God's Word, and ask Him to build these traits in our children's lives. As you read each day, write down specific requests concerning your children and family that God brings to mind as you record the Scripture verse that inspired your request. Then leave space to record God's answers.[1]

Personalize your prayers by putting your child's name in a passage. For example, I have prayed for Justin and each of our children from Ephesians 1:18, 19, "that the eyes of (his) heart may be enlightened so that (he) may know what is the hope of His calling, what are the riches of the glory of His inheritance in the saints, and what is the surpassing greatness of His power toward us who believe." I have found that when I do this, fear and anxiety leave me and are replaced by peace, confidence, and increased faith in God's promises. (See the end of this chapter for some suggested scriptures to pray for your children.)

WHEN TWO OR MORE ARE GATHERED: PRAYING WITH A PARTNER OR GROUP

Jesus tells us in Matthew 18:20 that when two or more people are gathered in His name, He is with them. It helps to find a partner to pray with. There is a special bond that forms from praying with someone else for our children. Whether it is your spouse, friend, sister, or Bible study member, enlist someone who is like-minded and believes in the power of prayer.

Several years ago in Vancouver, Washington, three parents were overwhelmed about the problems in their schools, so they committed themselves to pray together weekly and did so for three years. Eventually, as Wendy Flint was running for the school board, she met these parents who had prayed so diligently for God's intervention in their children's schools. They felt she and other Christians running for office and getting involved were the answer to their prayers, and would work for the very changes the group had been praying about for three years.

Virginia, a California mother, was concerned about the negative direction her children's schools were headed—the gangs, objectionable material in the curriculum, and problems in the classroom. She had been praying alone about the schools and had become discouraged. "The high school was right across the street from our house, and I could look out my front window and see throngs of teens wearing gang-related clothing, slouching near the school-yard gates, which looked to me like the gates of hell," says Virginia.

She resigned herself to praying alone, often walking around the entire perimeter of the high school with her dog, praying as she went. But she saw little change in the school and was disheartened.

In 1989, when both her children were in high school, Virginia had long forgotten to look for another mom to pray with. She kept a lonely vigil, often walking over to the Friday night football games to see her daughter march in with the flag team and to pray for the safety of the young people. One evening as she walked home from the football field across the student parking lot with her dog, she felt heavily burdened for all the students and prayed fervently for their safety. An hour or so later, when the game was over, a gang fight broke out in the parking lot and gun shots were fired through the crowd. However, not one student was hurt, and a security guard was only grazed on the arm when shot at close range.

About that time, Virginia heard a broadcast about Moms in Touch. What an encouragement for her to realize that there had been *thousands* of moms praying with her all the time! She got busy praying for another mom to join with—this time *knowing* that there was a partner out there somewhere. Soon she was invited to attend the high school Moms in Touch meeting by the mother who started the group.

This past year as the little group gathered and prayed, they saw many wonderful changes come about. The gangs were completely eliminated from their high school. Evolution was deleted from the biology curriculum due to "lack of time to cover everything in the text," as the science teacher explained The principal called the mothers and asked for prayer for a severely injured student. The student, who at first was not expected to live, awakened from a coma, made a speedy recovery, and was eager to play football again. The mothers have also built good relationships with teachers, counselors, and staff of all three schools—high school, middle school, and elementary.

"The new school year started off with the news that our elementary school had a new principal—a Christian!" says Virginia. "On September 11th at 7:00 A.M., I looked out my window at the high school across the street, and I saw 16 students gathered at the flag pole to pray, just inside the fence that three years earlier had looked to me like the gates of hell. As they bowed their heads in the morning mist, the sun shone through the trees and bounced off the walk leading into the school, lighting up the campus and leaving the walkways glistening. With that indelible picture in mind and the awareness of how far the Lord has brought us, I can only thank Him for softening my heart and opening my eyes to see what He can do through prayer."

"For the weapons of our warfare are not of the flesh, but divinely powerful for the destruction of fortresses. We are destroying speculations and every lofty thing raised up against the knowledge of God" (2 Cor. 10:4-5).

Instead of worrying, complaining, or running scared, thousands of mothers like Virginia are praying every week in Moms in Touch groups in every state and more than 85 countries—for their children, teachers, administration, and school districts. And answers to prayer have ranged from abstinence-based sex education curricula being chosen, to teachers becoming Christians and starting their own prayer and Bible study groups. For information on existing groups in your community or to order a leader's guide, materials to start a group, or the Moms in Touch video, call (800) 949-MOMS. You can also visit the Moms in Touch Web site (which has a new devotional every week) at: www.europa.com/~philhow/moms_in_touch.html.

THE BEGINNING OF MOMS IN TOUCH

Moms in Touch was founded in the fall of 1984, while Fern Nichols and her family were living in Abbotsford, British Columbia. That fall, Fern's two boys were entering junior high school, and she was concerned about all the pressures they would face. The burden to intercede for her boys was so overwhelming that she knew she could not bear it alone. Fern asked God to give her another mom to pray with concerning their children and their schools. She phoned another mom, who was enthusiastic. They thought of a few other mothers, called them, and began meeting every week for prayer. This was the beginning of Moms in Touch, International—mothers in touch with God, their children, their schools, and one another through prayer. Other groups sprang up in British Columbia from the elementary through high school levels. And when the Nichols family moved to Poway, California, the ministry began to spread throughout the United States and other countries.

These groups are having a quiet yet powerful impact on public schools. As a Michigan mom reports: "We have seen many, many answers to our prayers; it has been exciting! We have seen such a change in attitude at our school. Teachers who snickered at the thought of praying moms a year ago have grown to appreciate the thought." This past year, the teachers in their district worked without a contract, a matter of deep concern for the moms. Each week as they met, they prayed for contract settlement and each month they took a treat and note to the teachers, saying, "We're praying for you and appreciate you. Thanks for not letting contract talks affect your teaching." It really impressed the teachers that the mothers cared, encouraged them, and didn't condemn them as many in the community did.

In May, the contract was finally settled, and on May 9 the teachers had an Appreciation Tea to thank the Moms in Touch group for their support. Then to their further surprise, the school principal announced that the teachers had nominated them to receive the "Friends of Education" award by the St. Clair County's Educational Association. They were honored at a dinner and received an award plaque. Over and over that night, they heard educators say how wonderful it was to see moms involved and caring.

Besides praying, many Moms in Touch members volunteer in the classroom and serve in the school. Some groups also show appreciation to their school's faculty in creative ways throughout the year—remembering them and thanking them at holidays and special occasions with treats, notes of encouragement, and even new break room decor! One group inquired about the needs at the elementary school and found the teachers' break room was inadequate and gloomy. They asked about favorite colors and proceeded to paint all the walls, hang lovely pictures, add plants, and provide other spruce-ups. How greatly the teachers appreciated their surprise.

TWO BY TWO THOUSAND

Two by Two Thousand is a major prayer effort of the Christian Educators Association, a national support organization for Christian teachers serving in the public schools. Their goal is at least two teachers praying weekly in every school in the over 15,000 school districts in America by the year 2000.

In one such prayer partnership, two Connecticut teachers faithfully pray together every week. They pray for their principal, superintendent, fellow teachers, parents, and children. They pray about home situations that are difficult for their students. They include bus drivers and cafeteria workers in their prayers. They ask God for the grace to be salt and light in their classrooms and that others will be drawn to Christ because of His love in them. They encourage each other and are excited about how God is working in their school.

From the time our children were born, we have planted many

seeds in their lives—through our teaching, training, role modeling, loving, our involvement at school, and our parenting at home. Lamentations 2:19 says, "Pour out your heart like water before the presence of the Lord. Lift up your hands to Him for the life of your little ones." Let me encourage you to *water those seeds* with your prayers. God hears the prayers of a mom's, dad's, teacher's, and grandmother's heart for their children, and those prayers make a tremendous, eternal difference.

I believe God has a wonderful purpose for this generation of children and teenagers. Let's cooperate with His work by watering the seeds we've planted by praying for them, believing in them, and encouraging them, day after day.

SOME SUGGESTED SCRIPTURES TO PRAY FOR YOUR CHILD[3]

I pray that __________ will trust in the Lord with all his heart and not lean on his own understanding, that in all his ways he will acknowledge God and be directed by Him. (Proverbs 3:5-6)

I pray for the plans God has for __________, plans for welfare and not for calamity, to give him a future and a hope, and that he will let God work in his life to accomplish those plans. (Jeremiah 29:11)

I pray that ____________ will love the Lord with all their hearts and souls and might. (Deuteronomy 6:5)

I pray that ___________will grow to have the kind of love that is patient and kind, not jealous, arrogant, or boastful, never haughty or rude. (1 Corinthians 13:4-5)

I pray that God would surround __________with favor as with a shield. (Psalm 5:11-12)

I pray that ____________ would know that they can *always* turn to God, that His faithfulness is not dependent on their performance because He loves them with an everlasting love. (Psalm 62:5, 8)

I pray that ____________would be kind, tenderhearted, and forgiving. (Ephesians 4:32)

Since a child's friends have a tremendous impact, give ____________ the right friends who will encourage him to excel, and may he be kept from harmful friends who would lead him in the wrong direction. (Proverbs 2:20)

I pray that __________ would follow Christ and not stumble through the darkness, for living light that would flood his paths. (John 8:12)

I pray that God who began a good work in __________ will perform and bring it to completion. (Philippians 1:6)

CHAPTER 15

Becoming a Part of the Decision-Making Process

I am only one
But still I am one.
I cannot do everything.
But still I can do something.
And because I cannot do everything
I will not refuse to do the something
that I can do.
—Everett Hale[1]

The learning process of children must be a combined, total effort of teachers, parents, students, and administrators working together. We can't do everything, but each of us can do something to benefit the school our child attends.

We each have different interests and skills that affect what we have to offer as volunteers. It doesn't matter so much the form our involvement takes; what's important is finding a way to be involved at school that is right for us and sticking with it for the long haul.

I don't have the organizational or administrative talents to coordinate an all-school carnival (though I greatly admire those who do). Fund raising is not my forte, nor is serving as PTO president. I feel I can make my best contribution working directly with students in the classroom. For example, I can tutor children with their writing skills, spelling, and reading practice. For one year, I was a publishing volunteer and helped children edit and publish their own books. I also enjoy doing seminars for parents on how to support their child's learning at home.

Every mom and dad has something special to offer, and when you participate, everyone benefits—the children show more positive attitudes toward school, and teachers are able to offer programs, field trips, and learning opportunities that otherwise would not be possible. They can teach more effectively and better serve the individual needs of the child.

Parents benefit too: By being in the classroom, you know what your children are being taught and what they need to master, you see ways you can extend your child's learning at home, and you become more understanding of teachers and more aware of the problems schools face. Some parents serve on school-improvement committees to tackle those problems and find solutions. When you merely complain about what the school is doing, you lose credibility and respect, but when you serve as Christ served, you build a foundation for teachers and administrators to respect and listen to you.

PARENTS FILLING GAPS

When budget cuts forced a California elementary school to eliminate art, physical education, and after-school programs, parents began to serve as library and classroom aides, field trip drivers, chaperones, and playground supervisors. Other parents, who couldn't volunteer because of work schedules, helped by raising funds for needed supplies, computers, and programs or ran the Saturday school carnival. Today, the school has more than 350 parent volunteers for its 800 students, and nearly 550 families belong to a Home and School Club that has raised more than $35,000 for the school.

Northview Elementary in Manhattan, Kansas, is another good example of a school that benefits from parents' pitching in. Northview was honored as one of the four top elementary schools in the nation, and Principal Dr. Dan Yunk says a major reason for the school's success is *parent involvement.* Parents help in every area of the school, from running a "Clothing Rendezvous" (a clothing exchange) for all the children in the school, to working in the classroom and serving on school-improvement committees. In fact, all four of the top schools in the U.S. shared the characteristic that *parents are considered critical to the success of the school.* "If parents get involved, it improves the performance of the kids and the effectiveness of the school," says Dr. Yunk. Studies show parental involvement has much more influence on a student's achievement than other variables, such as class size, dollars spent, and teacher education.

In order to effectively involve parents, not just with a token program but with parents really participating, PTA's and improvement committees can suggest that schools need to:

- Tap the hidden talents of parents. One way is to send

out a sheet that invites participation and gives parents a wide variety of options. Follow-up should ensure that every parent who offers help has a chance to use his or her skills.

- Make parents feel welcome. Roll out the red carpet. Have a bright WELCOME poster in the entry, and make the school accessible to parents by providing a map on the bulletin board.
- Plan an orientation session for parent volunteers, and appoint a parent to be the Volunteer Coordinator.
- Train teachers how to work effectively with parents, since many have an "I can do it myself" attitude or cringe at the thought of parents in the classroom.

In Waco, Texas, parents have organized grandparents and senior citizens from the community to volunteer as classroom aides. "We have a retired colonel who comes in every morning from 8:30 to 10:00 to grade papers for the teacher," says Kris Olsen, PTA president. "He is on crutches and in poor health, but he has established a delightful relationship with the children. Every day he chooses a different student to compliment for improvement. The parents and teachers are planning a cooperative gardening project between the school and one of their adopted school partners, a senior citizens' garden club. They will have a fall and spring garden; the older children will work on square footage, fractions, and science projects with the gardeners."

Fathers, too, need to participate regularly in their children's education and find ways to become involved at school. More dads than ever before are becoming PTO officers and classroom aides and are serving on school boards, textbook committees, and in different capacities at school.

INNOVATIVE PARENTS

Sometimes Mom or Dad may volunteer for an activity, which later develops into an innovative program. After volunteering in her child's classroom, Katherine Newman, a Washington mother and Moms In Touch leader, realized that many children get so little reading practice at home that their reading skills slip further below grade level each year. So Katherine designed a read-aloud program to encourage reading at school, and she recruited and trained volunteers who work in 30-minute time slots. A large number of these reading volunteers are working parents who go to work 30 minutes to an hour late or come in at lunch to participate. And the children's reading skills are rising.

A California mother signed up as a playground aide after learning that fewer than 20 percent of California fifth-graders could pass a minimum fitness test. Because the school's P.E. program had been canceled, she developed a physical fitness program and a lunchtime recreation period.

Another parent I know wanted to boost the children's enthusiasm for reading the classics and discussing ideas, so she started a "Great Books" read-and-discuss group in her son's elementary school. Parents have also started and manned art and drama programs and taught foreign language classes that the school couldn't provide. A dad started a support group for parents whose child, like his, struggled with Attention Deficit Disorder and brought in speakers to show them how they could help at home. The sky's the limit when parents offer their skills and talents.

WORKING PARENTS PARTICIPATING IN SCHOOLS

It's important for working parents to have opportunities to help with school. "Employers must become sensitive to parents' needs to confer with teachers and to be actively involved with their children's education," said Dr. Carol Kelly, a school psychologist in the Jefferson County Colorado schools. "Employers already give time off to support the justice system with leave for jury duty. Is our educational system no less important? How about granting a few days a year for parents to work in the classroom? Encourage your employees to become active in the public schools. Allow them time off to visit their child's classrooms. Give sabbaticals for those who want to teach or help manage schools and offer management training for employees who plan to serve on school boards." [2]

If you are a supervisor, be as flexible as you can with employees' schedules so they can participate in their children's schools. If you're not, make every effort to convince your boss to support education by encouraging parent participation. Maybe even give him/her a copy of this book.

For working parents, remember, you don't have to do everything. Just pick one thing you can do and stick with it. Over the year's time, that will give you the opportunity to see the children, meet other parents, and get to know teachers.

Working parents say they find it more fulfilling and enjoyable to have direct contact with students in the time they do have to volunteer. If you have very little time, it might be best spent helping in the classroom with the children (rather than cutting out bulletin board figures and letters in the teacher's workroom). Let the teacher know, "I really want to participate and I don't have a lot of time, but I'm available for these hours. How can I help?" You'll need to plan in advance, but field trips might be your best place to participate.

If you can take at least one vacation day from work during the school year, let the teacher know you would love to participate in a school outing during the year. Ask her to let you know early enough for you to schedule the time off. For another field trip the class takes, check with the teacher to see if you could send some cupcakes or a fruit drink for each child to take along.

Or perhaps you could participate in an evening program. One school ran a once-a-week evening art program, in which working parents participated in projects and accompanied the children on a special outing to an art museum later in the month. Another held an annual "Stargazing, Storytelling, and Pizza Night" in which both working and at-home parents participated.

Here's a list of many different ways parents can enhance their child's education and help out at school, whether it's once a week, once a month, or once a semester. Pick something that fits with your skills, schedule, and interests:

- Put up bulletin boards.
- Do extra typing or duplicating.
- Be a library or media center aide to check in, laminate, and shelve books, help students find materials for reports, assist with displays, organize magazines, and repair books. The library is a great place for book lovers to volunteer, and you also discover the broad sampling of books, magazines, and resources in the school library.
- Help with fund-raising projects, such as carnivals, bake sales, school book fairs, etc.
- Help with special events, such as author visits, by arranging transportation for the author, planning meals, or videotaping presentations.
- Type and do layout work for the student newspaper or an anthology of student writing and artwork.
- Be a mentor to a child who needs special attention.

- Help with flower planting and landscaping around school.
- Drive or accompany children on field trips.
- Share your career expertise to extend the curriculum and help children develop goals for the future.
- Share your cultural knowledge by showing slides of travel, special memories, and information.
- Plan class parties or bring treats for special days.
- Start a "Living Social Studies" program: Invite each child's family for a 30-minute visit to share their hobbies and work or family history.
- Serve as a cafeteria or playground aide at lunchtime (this offers great opportunity to interact with and encourage children).
- Provide tutorial assistance.
- Join or form a read-and-discuss program with children: Parents read aloud to class, volunteer to listen to children, or read one-on-one or in groups.
- Serve as a volunteer in the student computer lab, and provide computer instruction, remedial instruction, and practice in basic skills.
- Find inspirational or motivational speakers in the community—athletes and people in business or service careers who are good role models—for assemblies.
- Serve as a public relations chairman. Take pictures of special events, reading contests, etc., and send them to your local newspaper to let the community know what's going on and to encourage participation. Judy, who is chairman of the public relations committee of her son's school, writes and sends press releases to the local newspaper about happenings, such as Red Ribbon Week (a drug-free

program). She made a video of the school to show to prospective parents, students, and the community.

- Organize an "Unplug the TV Week" for the school or your child's class to encourage families to watch less television. For how-to suggestions, check Marie Winn's *Unplugging the Plug-In Drug: Help Your Children Kick the TV Habit.*[3]
- Be in charge of videotaping daytime and evening school presentations, plays, and musical events so that parents who are unable to attend can see their child perform (video can be checked out in school library).
- Coordinate and lead a Moms in Touch group for your school.
- Coordinate a parent support network that provides assistance in stressful situations, such as when a mother dies or is seriously ill, when a chronically ill child has several surgeries, or when a family is homeless due to a fire.
- Assist school staff members in sponsoring after-school clubs.
- Serve on a committee to brainstorm and implement plans for improving education at school. At Manhattan, Kansas' Northview Elementary, 17 parents and community members help chart the future direction of the school.

THE SCHOOL BOARD AND YOUR CHILD'S EDUCATION

The school board is vitally important to you and your children because it decides virtually all policies of the district: hiring of the superintendent, establishing student learning objectives and student activity policies, selecting textbooks and curriculum, adopting and reviewing budgets, and much more.

But school board elections have been almost forgotten, and many parents do not even know who serves on their local school board. The average turnout for school board elections is 2-15 percent of voters in the over 15,000 school districts in America. And only 2 percent of American parents ever attend a school board meeting.[4]

When parents don't attend these meetings, board members don't hear what their concerns are. Parents then lose local control of their children's education. But when parents get active, find out how board members stand on issues, and are vocal about their concerns, the school board can become more responsive to parents.

To become aware and active with the school board, first *find out when your school board election is held*. Next, *find out what each candidate and incumbent board member represents*. Call and ask questions on issues that are important to you, such as: Do you believe sex education classes should begin at kindergarten? If not, at what grade level? Should sex education be mandatory or by parent permission only? Do you support "educational choice plans" for public schools? (See Appendix H for more questions to ask school board candidates.)

You can also attend school board meetings. Carolyn and Carl Curtis regularly attend school board meetings in their Michigan community. A TV channel offered each classroom seven minutes of news daily; however, the program included commercials. The Curtises' felt that once Channel 1 got into the school, parents would have no control over the types of commercials shown. They investigated Channel 1 before the meeting and presented the information to the school board members. Because of the Curtises' actions, their district was the only one in the county that did not implement Channel 1.

"We know that keeping in touch with our school board is vital to what happens in our school and district," says Lin Smith of San Diego, California. "We have set up an informal network of Christians who take turns attending the monthly meetings. We have two mothers who keep a close watch on the published agendas and notify others if there are items that need our attention. We have an informal 'phone tree' in several key churches to alert people to attend specific board meetings as necessary. This is how we got the school district to review the sex ed curriculum."

Running for school board may not be your cup of tea, but you can help those candidates you support by praying for them, having a meeting for people in the community to get to know them, or sponsoring a forum where all candidates can express their position and answer questions on the issues.

If you are led to ask questions or testify on an issue before the school board, do it graciously, in a businesslike way, and bring information, statistics, and support for your position (a spouse or another parent). "People often don't think their testimony is important, but *one* person speaking the truth can move a school board to vote in a different direction," says Wendy Flint. "We are responsible to speak out in a calm and logical manner and not to give up standing for what we know is right. If the vote doesn't go the way we wanted, we can know we did our part and leave the results in God's hands.

"Before sex education and drug education programs are adopted, before new literature or science curricula is funded, parents need to have a voice in their school board decisions," she continues.

"We can look closely at a board's proposal for implementing multicultural programs in a district and make sure it doesn't remove the teaching of American heritage or love of country and free enterprise. Students need to have a solid understanding of their own country's culture before they can begin to understand someone else's. Students should not be taught the values, philosophies, or politics of another culture at the expense of their own."

TAKING ACTION

Following are ways you can be involved in the decision-making processes in your child's school:

- Serve on a textbook-review committee. Call your local Board of Education office to find out about getting involved in the review process. "I frequently see notices in our San Diego newspaper seeking textbook reviewers," says Lin Smith.
- Join a parent-teacher organization. PTOs and PTAs are the most effective vehicle for informing parents of school issues. Parent-teacher organizations have traditionally been involved in sponsoring fund-raising events to pay for special programs and equipment that are not in the school budget; the PTA may coordinate volunteer activities, organize support and action groups, publish an informational newsletter, and sponsor parent-education programs. One PTA group organized and funded after-school enrichment activities for children in woodworking, calligraphy, dance, clowning and juggling, and "Super Study Skills," that gave children opportunities to develop their talent and interests. While serving on the PTA, you can have even more influence. You also become familiar with the school personnel and the administrative system at your child's school.
- Serve on a school committee to represent parent concern, such as staff development, at-risk committee, etc.

- Sponsor assemblies and programs through a parent organization. The Black Mountain Middle School PTSA researched, organized, and paid for a Bill Jones assembly, part of Josh McDowell's "Why Wait" campaign. The assembly was a big hit with students and staff.

  Students involved with Mt. Carmel Student Venture went to their advisor to recommend a school-wide assembly by Jacob Aranza, a nationally known youth speaker. The advisor turned them down four times, but the students and Moms in Touch kept praying for the assembly. Then "out of the blue" the advisor called and wanted more information on Aranza. Finally, Mt. Carmel held its first school-wide assembly in 10 years. All 3,600 students heard Jacob Aranza speak on abstinence in two assemblies. That same night an evangelistic rally in which over 250 students participated was held in a nearby auditorium.
- Give positive feedback in writing. After an event, such as the one mentioned, is held at your school, there may be negative criticism, and it takes many positives to overcome one negative. Sending a thank-you note and sharing how positively the event or speaker impacted your child helps the administrators know you appreciated their efforts and paves the way for similar events.

ONE PERSON CAN MAKE A DIFFERENCE

On Carl Rehberg's business card is his watchword: "One person can make a difference." It's a saying he has lived out. For the first year his daughter was in the Sioux Falls, South Dakota, public schools, Carl offered to help in the classroom. However, he never received a response. He also offered to help with the community education program and filled out an extensive form detailing his experience and expertise but received no feedback or invitation to help. Later, when a note was sent home to parents seeking input for a new mission statement for the school, Carl submitted a carefully thought out statement, but again heard nothing from school officials. The next year he volunteered to do anything to help. Still he got no response.

Carl had some real concerns about the school. He realized that other parents were looking for ways to help, and their efforts at involvement had been resisted. In his community, there were no associations where parents could express concerns or contribute ideas or recommendations. There were merely school-community councils run by principals for fund-raising and to bring in programs. Carl organized a meeting for parents interested in getting involved in the schools and nearly 90 people showed up to discuss the importance of parent involvement and the need to participate long term, not just for a cause or current issue. This core group became the Douglas Parents' Association, with its main objectives being "to serve the best interests of children by strengthening the role of parents in the educational system and building a renewed respect for parent and community involvement," to replace apathy with involvement, promote quality education, and serve and support the children, teachers, and schools through volunteerism, projects, and purchase of needed items. They created a constitution and by-laws and a monthly newsletter, and they sought practical ways to serve.

The parents' association came up with a homework contract and encouraged parents to sign it and implement it at home. The contract had specific goals for the child and support by the parent, and gave helpful hints for parents to use at home to help their child be more successful in school. The association started thinking about the next school board election and wanted to introduce a strong parent involvement stance (although they didn't run a candidate). In conjunction with the League of Women Voters, they held a forum where the candidates could speak to voters about their platform and let parents ask questions. This public forum for the school board election was a first in this community. Parents got to interact with candidates and find out where they stood on important issues. They also encouraged community members to vote in the upcoming election. Previously only 2-3 percent of people on the Ellsworth Air Force Base had voted in this election, although they had 80 percent of the children in the schools.

Through their efforts, a candidate who favored increased parent involvement was elected. That member initiated a public seminar (with the U.S. Under Secretary of Education from the Department of Education as guest speaker who spoke on "Parent/Community Involvement for Education"). At that meeting, Carl distributed a new school board policy proposal for strong parental involvement and sought feedback from parents, teachers, and school board members. Several weeks later, with the proposed changes made, the association presented the policy to the school board. The new Parental/Community Involvement Policy statement, which the school board recently approved, includes much of the material proposed by the Douglas Parents' Association.

Because of the efforts of Carl and the Douglas Parents' Association, a bill ensuring abstinence education and character education was passed and signed into law in 1992, as well as other reforms that affected schools statewide.

Lin Smith's daughter had attended a Christian school for two years. When the Smith family moved to California and enrolled their children in a public school, Lin joined the PTA and began a Moms in Touch group. She served as Hospitality Chairman of the PTA and planned the "Welcome Back" luncheon for teachers, holiday snacks for the teacher's room, the Teacher Appreciation breakfast, and other events. Although the Smiths were a "new family on the block," Lin showed she cared about building a better school.

At the end of that year, the sex education curriculum was introduced, first with a parent review night, and then in the eighth-grade classrooms. The Smiths judged the material as acceptable. However, when the sex education program was presented in the classroom, "safe sex" rather than abstinence was taught, and students were encouraged to participate in controversial practices that had not been presented at the parents' meeting.

At the next PTA meeting, Lin asked questions about the program and discussed her concerns with the teacher and principal. They listened to her because of her previous school involvement. She prayed with the Moms in Touch group that this school would send parents and staff members to a Sex Respect training seminar. After presenting the idea to the school, Lin, the PTA mom in charge of health issues, the school counselor, and a teacher were sent to the seminar on abstinence-based sex education programs for schools.

Following their training, they presented the program to the principal and PTA, who asked them to show it to the school board. However, at that level, the person in charge of curriculum strongly rejected the Sex Respect program and indicated that the school would not consider changing the sex education curriculum.

Soon after, through the efforts of parents from all over California, the legislature passed a bill stating that all sex education must be taught from an abstinence perspective. The state gave school districts one year to comply with the legislation. Now with the legal muscle they needed, those supporting abstinence-based programs showed the district that the current curriculum violated the state requirements.

You, too, can have an impact on your child's education, help him make the most of school, and equip him to bloom academically and spiritually.

As a result of this five-year-long process, the sex education textbooks for middle schools and high schools were replaced with abstinence-based materials. Teachers are now prohibited from using supplemental materials that conflict with the abstinence-based approach.

Lin's involvement changed not only her child's school but also the whole district. You, too, can have an impact on your child's education, help him make the most of school, and equip him to bloom academically and spiritually.

CHAPTER 16

Putting Computers to Use at Home and School

Computers can tap into your child's interest and provide challenging learning opportunities, make home learning exciting, improve writing skills, and even facilitate researching for reports and projects. But as with all other aspects of your child's schooling, *your involvement* is the key.

When Richard and Penny Hook and their three children spent 18 months in Beijing, China, they wrote and transmitted 190 E-mail messages to their parents, siblings, and friends back in the U.S. Sitting in front of a computer screen, Richard and Penny related the extraordinary and the mundane, from passing through customs to exploring the Great Wall to trying to find a pharmacy.

When their once-in-a-lifetime trip was over, the Hooks bound all their E-mail messages (including 225 E-mail letters they received from Richard's family) into a special memory book called China Letters.

Today the China Letters journal is a vivid reminder that the world is getting smaller. "Our families knew what was going on in each other's lives almost on a daily basis, even though we were thousands of miles apart," says Richard.

What the Hooks tapped into was one of the safest and best educational uses of the computer: E-mail, or electronic mail, where you can send and receive messages through your home computer, using a modem and phone line. It's like sending and getting regular mail in your mailbox, but much faster! This computer equipment also allows you to browse through the Internet, the global network of computers linking universities, corporations, and government.

Some families are not aware that this burgeoning new technology can bring the world to their fingertips. Although more than 35 million American homes have personal computers with modems, many of these families are missing out on the uses that can benefit their children's learning.

The computer has much more potential than just playing games, killing enemies and escaping from villains' traps. There's software to create multimedia projects, aid in writing book reports, design graphics, and provide practical resources for day-to-day schoolwork. For example, you can call out spelling words while the child types each one in a word-processing program, then activate the spell check to see how he did. And while much has been said about the dangers of kids in cyberspace, a major way to safeguard your family is to take the time to learn the working of computers, modems, Internet software, and online services so you can monitor your child's use. That way, you can help your child employ the computer as something more than a video-game machine.

LAUNCHING INTO CYBERSPACE

What are some of the benefits of having a computer and modem in the home? The next time your children are assigned to report on the American Revolution, they can tap into the Library of Congress for a wealth of information. They can also E-mail a letter to the editor of a children's magazine they subscribe to, send thank-you letters to relatives, and develop a pen-pal friendship with a child or relative in another country.

When Oregon sixth-grader Andrew Tunnell's older brother spent a summer studying at a German university, they found E-mail an easy way to keep in touch. "Every other day we'd E-mail each other," Andrew reports. "My brother would tell me what castle he visited that day and some history about it." Not only did Andrew's typing and writing skills improve dramatically, but he also learned a lot of first-hand information about another country.

Children who learn to use the computer as a communications tool at home gain valuable language skills that help them achieve more in every subject. Since fluency and skill in writing are developed by practice, online activities provide many reasons to write at home—the place most kids write the least. But *your* involvement as a parent is essential, both to your child's safety online and to his learning how to tap into the best educational use of the technology.

When your children log on, here's how you can help them get the most out of their computer time:

1. Set guidelines and ground rules.

Just as it's important to set ground rules covering the content of your kids' TV viewing, so it's vital to set clear guidelines for their computer and Internet use. Tom Lough of Simsbury, Connecticut, allowed his son, Kyser, to E-mail a friend he met at summer camp, but he set some house rules: Ask for permission each time you log on; don't ever leave the "basic services" area of the online service; anything dealing with adult language is off-limits; and don't ever give out their password. He and his son moved from joint sessions in which he helped Kyser log on to Tom reading a book nearby and checking on Kyser periodically.

Tom also instructed Kyser not to give out any personal information, such as their home address or telephone number. Since E-mail travels over phone lines and through many computers, the messages could be read by strangers.

Besides these guidelines, keep in mind that it's also important to:

Set time limits. Just like watching too much TV, your children can spend too much time on the computer. Monitor the amount of time spent online, and make sure it's balanced with lots of other activities, including conversations with parents, study, reading, and play.

Be a mentor. Just as you wouldn't send your children to the movies or mall without some supervision and guidelines, don't turn them loose on the Internet either. Don't leave them to navigate cyberspace by themselves. Show them the proper way to turn the computer on and off and how to use the printer. Locate the computer in the family room or other common area, *not* a child's bedroom.

Set boundaries. Preview all new software, and if any games or other programs are unacceptable, draw the line. Monitor your children's use of the Internet, and purchase a program that blocks unacceptable or unsafe sites for kids (e.g., "Kid Desk") or use an Internet service like Integrity Online. Determine your standards for acceptable and unacceptable Web sites and games, and make sure your children know them.

2. Teach your children "netiquette."

Courtesy is just as important when writing E-mail letters as it is when talking in person. Discuss with your children these netiquette suggestions so they will practice politeness in print:

- Answer your E-mail promptly and politely, and in most cases, briefly.
- Address E-mail letters properly, using the person's correct title, such as "Dear Librarian" or "Dear Editor," and use an appropriate closing, such as "Sincerely, Kathy" or "Your friend, Brian."
- Don't write in ALL CAPITAL LETTERS—it's just like SHOUTING!
- Encourage your kids to use complete sentences and to end each sentence with a dot (keyboard term for a period).

3. Encourage activities that build literacy.

There's a lot of fun stuff to do online that gives children great opportunities to learn:

Tap into libraries. Meghan, a seventh-grader, did all her research for her report on Thomas Jefferson online. She was even able to download some historical documents from the Library of Congress to add to her resources.

After reading and discussing an important national issue together, E-mail your congressman. Check with the congressman's local office for E-mail addresses.

Have an E-mail pen pal. Your children can become connected with friends from summer camp or pen pals in other countries and learn about their cultures and the differences in their schools, families, and lifestyles. One of the best ways to find a safe online pen pal is to contact the missions organization your church is associated with and ask for E-mail addresses of missionary families. Your children can then correspond via E-mail with missionary kids, who would appreciate the friendship and support. Another way to find a safe online pen pal is for two schools to link up and exchange E-mail address of students interested in corresponding.

Create a family newsletter. Let your children be the news reporters and even interview Granddad and other relatives. Then they can write it all up and E-mail it to the whole family with a click of the "send" key.

4. Discover educational opportunities.

Each online service has sites where students can learn about everything from physics to a foreign language. For example, there are French- and German-only conferences where American students can practice those languages with students from France and Germany.

You can find educational sites such as those described above in resources like the *Internet Kids and Family Yellow Pages* (Osborne-McGraw-Hill), which comes out once a year and lists thousands of educational and family-friendly sites and safe learning sites for children.

5. Use E-mail to stay involved with your children's education.

Most schools have computers, and many have modems and are

online, allowing students, teachers, and parents to stay in close touch. Ask your children's teachers if they have an online address, and then correspond by E-mail to keep updated about what the class is studying. You can ask how your kids are doing and how you can work with them on problem areas.

Many universities now supply students with computers and free Internet access, so you can also keep up with what's going on with your college kids. While Kendall Hagan's son was at the U.S. Naval Academy in Annapolis, Maryland, the two kept in daily touch via E-mail, which gave him needed support from home.

You can read magazines such as *Family PC* and *Computers Made Easy (for Parents)* that keep you informed about issues such as: Internet safety; how to lay down rules for online use; recommendations on the best computer games and software for art or learning activities; and regular updates on Web sites children should avoid. To find good educational software, you can ask your children's teachers for recommendations, talk to other parents, read reviews in computer magazines, and visit publishers' Web sites and try free demos.

By getting on the information highway with your children and using E-mail yourself, you'll quickly get over your fear of the online world, set a good example, and at the same time effectively monitor your kids' computer use.

SCHOOLS, COMPUTERS, AND THE INTERNET

Computer and Internet use in the classroom have skyrocketed in recent years, causing concern among many parents. The information highway offers numerous benefits for classroom learning, but it's still important for parents to be informed and aware of how their kids are using computers at school.

So how *are* computers being employed? Math teachers have students do drills with programs like "Math Munchers," which challenges basic math operations with whole numbers, decimals, and fractions. Social studies and science teachers have students do research, depending on how many Internet hook-ups they have available. For example, while students work on science fair projects, they may use Word to type their hypothesis, procedure, data, and conclusion; they might use Excel to make graphs and charts with their collected data. They could research different European countries through the encyclopedia on CD ROM, make brochures on the desktop publishing program to put with their exhibits, and use word-processing software to type their reports.

In special-education or learning-disabled classrooms, students who have difficulty with handwriting can use the keyboard to type their work. Those who have trouble with spelling can take spelling tests on the computer and use the spell check feature when writing reports. Even students with low academic skill can use the computer's painting software for art projects and benefit from games that teach them to match objects and learn colors. Voice-activated programs assist children with cerebral palsy who can't write or type at all.

In addition, the use of electronic mail and the Internet have enabled teachers and students:

- to work on collaborative writing projects with classes in distant locations
- to exchange pen-pal messages with people from other cultures
- to link learners with experts such as cloud physicists and NASA scientists who can serve as mentors
- to compile worldwide survey data ranging from rain acidity and shopping costs to opinion polls

- to communicate directly via the Internet with people in the countries involved when the Gulf War and the breakup of the Soviet Union were taking place
- to participate in electronic "discussion groups" on topics of specific interest to students

Students can also do extensive research online, searching university libraries, art galleries, and news archives for information. They can check current events and learn about almost any subject. Since the Internet connects more than 46,000 computer networks worldwide, there are myriad possibilities for finding information. That's why many schools have jumped on the bandwagon and are providing Internet access for their teachers and students.

Nonetheless, children's use of the computer and Internet still needs to be monitored. How is that done? Supervision varies from school district to school district. In many, all Internet access is screened, for teachers as well as students, and district personnel as well as principals get a list every month of any attempts to reach inappropriate or off-limits sites. Some schools install programs like CyberPatrol that, when installed, will key in on certain words. If those words are used in a search, the program won't let the search go through. In other schools, parents and students sign a contract that spells out the rules for appropriate Internet use; misuse can then lead to suspension of Internet privileges. *The only way to know your school's policies and how much supervision is being provided is to ask.*

Here are six questions that Gateways to Better Education advises parents to ask teachers or administrators regarding the Internet in your children's schools:[1]

1. Does the school use some kind of Internet filtering software?
2. If not, what kind of adult supervision will there be while

students access the Internet? Will computer monitors be facing in a direction that allows an adult to easily and frequently see what's on the screen?

3. If there's to be no adequate adult supervision, or even when adult supervision is present, how will the school be held accountable if pornographic images or text are accessed by minors on school property?
4. How will the school guard against creating a hostile learning environment for students who may be working at a computer terminal next to a monitor that is being used to view pornographic images?
5. If the school takes no responsibility for the content of what students access on the Internet, is the school willing to extend this "hands off" policy to images and text that students print (and possibly distribute) from the pornographic sites? Will the school have this same policy regarding racist images and text?
6. If the school district takes no responsibility for pornographic images or text accessed by minors on school property, is the district truly willing to spend thousands of education dollars defending itself in potential lawsuits for (1) contributing to the delinquency of minors, (2) allowing a sexually hostile learning environment to exist on campus, and (3) allowing obscene material on campus?

BE INFORMED

As in every area of your children's education, it's important to be informed about the computer and Internet, both at home and at school. That way, you can help your kids learn and make the most of the technology. Ignorance is not bliss, especially when it comes to the computer! Kids often are far ahead of us parents in computer literacy. But with some self-education—perhaps a computer course at the local community center or having your children show you a thing or two on your home computer—you can make a difference and provide a good role model at the same time.

Endnotes

Introduction

1. Eric Buehrer, *Gateways to Better Education* newsletter, August 1997, p. 1.
2. Laurence Steinberg, Bradford Brown, and Sanford Dornbusch, *Beyond the Classroom: Why School Reform Has Failed and What Parents Need to Do* (New York: Simon & Schuster, 1996).

Chapter 1

1. Anne Henderson, "The Evidence Continues to Grow: Parent Participation and Student Achievement" (Columbia, MO: National Committee for Citizens in Education, 1981).
2. For information on Moms in Touch, see chapter 14.

Chapter 2

1. Connecticut, Georgia, Indiana, Kentucky, Maine, Missouri, New York, North Carolina, Oregon, South Carolina, and Texas.
2. Arizona, Arkansas, California, Colorado, Delaware, Idaho, Iowa, Massachusetts, Michigan, Minnesota, Nebraska, New Hampshire, New Jersey, North Dakota, Ohio, Tennessee, Utah, and Washington.
3. Colorado, Florida, Georgia, Idaho, Maine, Massachusetts, Minnesota, New Jersey, Ohio, Utah, Washington, and Wisconsin.
4. Arizona, Arkansas, Indiana, Kansas, Louisiana, Oklahoma, and Nevada.
5. I.K. Taylor, "Idaho to Allow Homeschoolers to Attend College Full-time," *Education Week*, April 2, 1997, p. 18.
6. Some of the states with charter school laws are Alaska, Arizona, Arkansas, California, Colorado, Connecticut, Delaware, Florida, Georgia, Hawaii, Idaho, Illinois, Kansas, Louisiana, Massachusetts, Michigan, Minnesota, Mississippi, Missouri, New Hampshire, New Jersey, New Mexico, North Carolina, Ohio, Pennsylvania, Rhode Island, South Carolina, Texas, Utah, Virginia, Wisconsin, and Wyoming.
7. Colorado, Idaho, Illinois, Iowa, Maine, New Hampshire, North Dakota, Utah, and Washington. In Steven McGarvey, "Can Homeschoolers

Participate in Public School Activities? A State-by-State Analysis," a paper distributed by the Home School Legal Defense Association, February 26, 1997, pp. 1-2.

8. Some of the cities in which scholarship programs exist include: AR: Little Rock. AZ: Phoenix. CA: Los Angeles and Oakland. CO: Denver. CT: Bridgeport. District of Columbia. FL: Orlando. GA: Atlanta. IL: Chicago. IN: Indianapolis. MI: Battle Creek, Detroit/Grand Rapids, and Jackson. NJ: Jersey City and Newark. NY: Albany, Buffalo, New York City, Washington Heights. OK: Oklahoma City. PA: Philadelphia and Pittsburgh. TN: Knoxville. TX: Austin, Dallas, Houston, Midland, San Antonio. WA: Seattle. WI: Milwaukee.
9. A tax *credit* can be applied to the total tax owed to the government. A tax *deduction* can only reduce the amount of money that will be taxed by the government.

Chapter 3

1. Arnold Burron, *Helping Kids Cope: A Parent's Guide to Stress Management* (Elgin, IL: David C. Cook, 1988), pp. 99-100.
2. Great Books Foundation, 40 East Huron Street, Chicago, IL 60611.
3. Cheri Fuller, "Your Child: Full of Promise," *Home-Life: The Key to Your Child's Success at School* (Tulsa, OK: Honor Books, 1988).

Chapter 4

1. See p. 180 for Focus on the Family film *Molder of Dreams*, featuring Guy Doud.
2. Burron, *Helping Kids Cope*, p. 94.
3. Author unknown.
4. Margie Golick, *Deal Me In* (New York: Monarch Press, Simon and Schuster, Inc., 1985), p. 4.
5. Burron, *Helping Kids Cope*, p. 96.

Chapter 5

1. My appreciation to school psychologist Carol Kelly of the Jefferson County, Colorado, schools for her input on parent-teacher collaboration.

2. Many elementary teachers send home a folder on Friday or another day of the week, enclosing all the child's marked-up or corrected work for the week and a comment/question sheet to be signed by the parent and returned on Monday. Don't pass up the opportunity to communicate to the teacher through this vehicle she's provided to stay in touch with your child's work, to say a word of thanks, or to express your concern about something your child doesn't understand.

Chapter 6

1. "How to Protect and Nurture Your Child While He Is in Public School," special report by Eric Buehrer (Lake Forest, CA: Gateways to Better Education, 1992).
2. Peter Marshall, *The Light and the Glory* (Old Tappan, NJ: Fleming H. Revell Co., 1977).
3. Buehrer, "How to Protect and Nurture Your Child While He Is in Public Schools."
4. Ibid.
5. Michael Ebert, "Liberals Malign Parents as 'Censors,' " *Focus on the Family Citizen*, Dec. 16, 1991, p. 5.
6. "How to Appeal School Actions" information sheet, by National Committee for Citizens in Education.
7. Carolyn also suggests a six-book series she used to prepare herself to talk confidently and clearly with her children about sex throughout their growing up years. The series is called *Learning About Sex*, published by Concordia Publishing (rev. ed. 1988, St. Louis, MO). This is for ages three and up and includes a parent guidebook.
8. From the Josh McDowell series *Why Wait?* written by Bill Jones and Barry St. Clair, Here's Life Publishers, San Bernardino, CA, 1987.
9. *Understanding the Times* (Summit Ministries, P.O. Box 207, Manitou Springs, CO 80829).
10. From comments by Jeff Myers, Summit Ministries.
11. Eric Buehrer, *Gateways to Better Education* newsletter, August 1997, p. 3.
12. *Of Pandas and People*, The Foundation for Thought and Ethics, Book Project Chairman and Academic Editor, Dr. Charles B. Thaxton (Dallas: Houghton Publishing Co., 1989).

Chapter 7

1. Arnold Burron, *Helping Kids Cope: A Parents' Guide to Stress Management* (Elgin, IL: David C. Cook), pp. 95-96.
2. James Dobson, *The New Dare to Discipline* (Wheaton, IL: Tyndale House Publishers, 1992).
3. James Dobson, *Parenting Isn't for Cowards* (Dallas: Word Publishers, 1997).
4. Stephen Arterburn and Jim Burns, *Parents Guide to Top 10 Dangers Teens Face* (Colorado Springs: Focus on the Family, 1995).

Chapter 8

1. Judge Randall Hekman, from *Homemade*, Vol. 12, No. 10, Oct. 1988 published by Family Concern, Wheaton, IL.
2. Ted W. Engstrom, *The Pursuit of Excellence* (Grand Rapids, MI: Zondervan, 1982) paraphrased.
3. Larry Burkett, "Motivated by Purpose," *How to Manage Your Money*, a newsletter of Christian Financial Concepts, Gainesville, GA, p. 5.

Chapter 9

1. Faith Clark, *Hassle-Free Homework* (New York: Doubleday, 1989), pp. 41-42.
2. Cheri Fuller, *Unlocking Your Child's Learning Potential* (Colorado Springs, CO: NavPress, 1994).

Chapter 10

1. Rudolf Flesch, *Why Johnny Still Can't Read: A New Look at the Scandal of Our Schools* (New York: Harper & Row, 1981).
2. Ibid., p. 123.
3. Using his own experience, Tony's dad, Dr. Carl Smith, a professor at Indiana University, founded Parents Sharing Books. Over 300 parents and their middle-school-age students in 20 Indiana schools are now reading books together and talking about them. For information write: Parents Sharing Books, Family Literacy Center, 2805 E. 10th St., Bloomington, IN 47405.
4. Adapted from Cheri Fuller's book *Teaching Your Child to Write* (New York: Berkley Books, 1997).

5. "What Works: Research About Teaching and Learning," William J. Bennett, former Secretary of Education, U.S. Dept. of Education, 1986.

Chapter 11

1. Boston Museum of Science, Science Park, Boston, MA 02114-1099, (800) 729-3300 or (617) 589-0437.
2. Insect Lore Products, P.O. Box 1535, Shafter, CA 93263, (800) LIVE-BUG.
3. Richard Phillips Feynman, *Surely You're Joking, Mr. Feynman* (New York: Bantam Books, 1985).
4. For more information on tree planting, write Global Releaf Program, P.O. Box 2000, Washington, D. C. 20013.
5. Recycle aluminum cans, foil, pie plates, and frozen food trays. Recycling aluminum cuts related air pollution by 98 percent.
6. It is vital to cut the six-pack plastic rings into pieces because they are invisible in the water. Birds are choked and strangled by them; fish and animals get their heads in the rings and die.
7. Gary Bauer and Dr. James Dobson, *Children at Risk* (Dallas: Word Books, 1990) p. 189.

Chapter 12

1. Perry L. Glanzer, *Virtue 101: The Strengths and Limitations of Character Education in Public Schools*, Focus on the Family Public Policy Division, 1998, p. 16.
2. Ibid.

Chapter 13

1. Bill Mattox, Jr., "Children Need More Time with Parents," *Colorado Springs Gazette Telegraph*, March 10, 1991, D3.
2. Jeff suggests a booklet titled "How to Stand Alone," a guide parents can use to teach their families to stand for Christ in difficult circumstances. Available from The Institute for Basic Life Principles, P.O. Box 1, Oak Brook, IL 60522.
3. Appreciation to Jeff Myers for his ideas on ways parents can serve.
4. Zorach v. Clauson, 343 U. S., 1952.

5. Most RTCE programs have a board of directors with representatives of each church in the community; they are encouraged to avoid denominational differences.

Chapter 14

1. Jean Fleming, *A Mother's Heart* (Colorado Spring: NavPress, 1982), p. l.
2. Fern Nichols "Moms in Touch" (Poway, CA: 1987), pp. 3-4.
3. Suggested prayers are based on scriptures from NIV and NASB Bibles.

Chapter 15

1. *Bartlett's Familiar Quotations* (Boston: MA: Little Brown & Co., 1980 15th ed.).
2. From the author's interview with Dr. Kelly.
3. Marie Winn, *Unplugging the Plug-In Drug: Help Your Children Kick the TV Habit* (New York: Viking Press, 1987).
4. Wendy Flint, "School Boards: A Call to Action," American Parents Association.

Chapter 16

1. My thanks to Eric Buehrer, Gateways to Better Education, for his suggestions. See Appendix A for more information.

Appendix A

RESOURCE ORGANIZATIONS

American Center for Law & Justice
P.O. Box 64429
Virginia Beach, VA 23467
(757) 226-2489
www.aclj.org

Association of American Educators
26012 Marguerite Parkway, #333
Mission Viejo, CA 92692
www.aaeteachers.org

Christian Education Association International
P.O. Box 41300
Pasadena, CA 91114
(626) 798-1124
www.ceai.org

Christian Legal Society
4208 Evergreen Lane, Suite 222
Annandale, VA 22003
(703) 642-1070
www.clsnet.com

Family Research Council
801 G Street, NW
Washington, DC 20001
(202) 393-2100
www.frc.org

Fellowship of Christian Athletes
8701 Leeds Road
Kansas City, MO 64129
(816) 921-0909
www.fca.org

Focus on the Family
Colorado Springs, CO 80995
(719) 531-3400 or
(800) A-FAMILY to order resources
www.family.org

Foundation for Thought and Ethics
P.O. Box 830721
Richardson, TX 75083
(800) 669-3410

Gateways to Better Education
P.O. Box 514
Lake Forest, CA 92630-0514
(888) 929-1163
www.gtbe.org

Moms in Touch, International
P.O. Box 1120
Poway, CA 92074-1120
(800) 949-MOMS
www.europa.com/~philhow/moms_in_touch.html

National Association for Released Time Christian Education
5722 Lime Avenue
Long Beach, CA 90805
(800) 360-7943

Probe Ministries
1900 Firman Drive, Suite 100
Richardson, TX 75081
(972) 480-0240
www.probe.org

See You at the Pole
12335 World Trade Drive, Suite 16
San Diego, CA 92128
(619) 592-9200
www.syatp.com
Student Discipleship Ministries
www.studentdiscipleship.org

Student Venture
Campus Crusade for Christ
100 Sunport Lane
Orlando, FL 32809
(800) 789-5462
http://www.ccci.org/student_venture

Summit Ministries
P.O. Box 207
Manitou Springs, CO 80829
(719) 685-9103
www.summit.org

The Light Club (prayer groups for children in public schools)
Karen Moran, President
P.O. Box 210384
West Palm Beach, FL 33421
(561) 478-8361 (phone & fax)
E-mail: KMORAN98@aol.com

Young Life International
P.O. Box 520
Colorado Springs, CO 80901
(719) 473-4262
www.younglife.org

Youth for Christ
P.O. Box 228822
Denver, CO 80222
(303) 843-9000
www.gospelcom.net/yfc

Appendix B

BOOKS AND BOOKLETS

Creating a Positive Public School Experience, Eric Buehrer (Thomas Nelson, 1994)

Facts, Not Fear, Michael Sanera & Jane Shaw (Regnery Press, 1996)

The New Hide or Seek, James Dobson (Revell, 1979)

Knowing Your Rights, Jay Allen Sekulow (American Center for Law and Justice, 1996). See ACLJ organizations to order.

Parenting Isn't for Cowards, James Dobson (Word, 1997)

Preparing for Adolescence, James Dobson (Tyndale, 1992)

Religion and American Education: Rethinking a National Dilemma (University of North Carolina Press, 1995)

Student Rights and the Public Schools, Jay Allen Sekulow (American Center for Law and Justice, 1995)

Teaching Your Child to Write, Cheri Fuller (Berkley, 1997)

The Closing of the American Heart: What's Really Wrong with America's Schools, Ronald H. Nash (Probe Books, 1990)

The Teacher-Reacher Packet. Materials from Gateways to Better Education designed to help you build a better relationship with your child's teacher and share Christ's love with her. Packet includes three holiday restoration cards, two encouragement note cards, a prayer log to pray for classroom, and a parent-teacher conference checklist. Order from (800) 929-1163 or (888) 706-5601.

365 Ways to Develop Your Child's Values; 365 Ways to Build Your Child's Self-Esteem; 365 Ways to Help Your Child Learn, all by Cheri Fuller (NavPress, 1994)

Unlocking Your Child's Learning Potential, Cheri Fuller (NavPress, 1994)

When Children Pray, Cheri Fuller (Multnomah, 1998)

When Mothers Pray, Cheri Fuller (Multnomah, 1997)

World-Proofing Your Kids: Helping Moms Prepare Their Kids to Navigate Today's Turbulent Times, Lael Arrington (Crossway, 1997)

Appendix C

BOOKS, RESOURCES, AND ORGANIZATIONS

Sex Education

"A Message to Teens About Sex" (Fran Sciacca)
This "Focus on the Family" broadcast cassette focuses on relationships and the consequences of sexual involvement. The God-given differences between the sexes, the value of modesty, setting boundaries, and establishing respect are addressed.

Decent Exposure, by Connie Marshner (Adroit Press)
Insights on how to teach children about modesty, premarital dating, and marriage are offered in this book. Creating a healthy sexual foundation is the key to establishing right attitudes and moral absolutes.

Foundations for Family Life Education, by Margaret Whitehead and Onalee McGraw (Educational Guidance Institute)
A practical guide for parents of elementary, junior high, and high school students covering the topics of Family Life Education, contrasting models of sex education, and five foundations for successful family life education. To order, contact: Educational Guidance Institute, 188 Berbuse Lane, Front Royal, VA 22630. Phone: (540) 635-4420.

How to Help Your Child Say "No" to Sexual Pressure, by Josh McDowell (Here's Life)
This book equips parents and teens with practical "how to say no" principles as well as creative preventative measures to help teens withstand the pressures of premarital sexual activity.

National Guidelines for Character and Sexuality Education, by The Medical Institute for Sexual Health
Guidelines for parents, schools, and health professionals outlining an abstinence-centered approach to sex education. To order, contact: The Medical Institute for Sexual Health, P.O. Box 162306, Austin, TX 78716. Phone: (512) 328-6268; fax: (512) 328-6269.

Preparing for Adolescence, by James Dobson (Regal)
Dr. Dobson gives a powerful message to adolescents to help them understand the challenges of the teen years. The topics include self-esteem, peer pressure, physical changes, love, emotions, and the importance of sexual purity.

Raising Them Chaste, by Dr. Richard C. Durfield and Renee Durfield (Bethany)
The Durfields offer positive, assertive, and practical ways to motivate youth to remain chaste until marriage. Parents are encouraged to give their teen a ring or similar object as a token and constant reminder of the commitment.

"Straight Talk to Teens About Sex" (Joe White, James Dobson)
This Focus on the Family cassette contains letters and poems written by teens concerning the consequences of yielding to sexual pressure. Information is provided on "safe sex," promiscuity, emotions tied to abortion, and other related issues.

"The Many Myths of Safe Sex" I, II (Joe McIlhaney, James Dobson)
This Focus on the Family cassette provides updated information on the epidemic of sexually transmitted diseases in the U.S. occurring largely as a result of the "safe sex" myth. Dr. McIlhaney refutes the claim that condoms prevent HIV and other STDs.

"Understanding Physical and Sexual Development" I, II (James Dobson)
In this cassette from the "Preparing for Adolescence" album, Dr. Dobson explains to preadolescents some of the changes their bodies are going through.

God's plan for marriage, the sexual appetite, sexually transmitted diseases, and making wise decisions are among some of the topics discussed.

Weaving Character Into Sex Education, by Pat Socia
A workbook designed for parents, teachers, and students on the benefits of character education combined with sex education. The book details how character and virtue can be woven into the fabric of sex education and explains why it is the best method of solving the crisis of out-of-wedlock pregnancy, welfare reform, STDs, and the pain of broken relationships. To order, contact: Project Reality, P.O. Box 97, Golf, IL 60029-0097. Phone: (847) 729-3298.

When It's Time for the Talk, by Gayle Bucher
A book for parents that encourages and equips them to address the issue of sex education with their children. To order, contact: Creating Positive Relationships, 30 N. Rangeline Road, Suite A, Carmel, IN 46032. Phone: (317) 846-0386.

Audiovisual Resources on Teenage Sexuality

But Is It Safe?
Miles McPherson talks to young people about STDs, AIDS, abstinence, and condoms. This two-part video takes students through a lively, open, and honest question-and-answer session. Each tape runs 20 minutes in length.

No *Apologies: The Truth About Life, Love and Sex*
Dramatic vignettes illustrating teen experiences with sex, unwed pregnancy, and teen marriage are combined with clips of teens and medical authorities to encourage abstinence. Focus on the Family, Colorado Springs, CO 80995. Phone: (800) 932-9132.

Sexual Health Today
A slide presentation designed to educate parents, teens, teachers, and health workers on the most prevalent sexually transmitted diseases, the myths of safe sex, and the safest form of protection against STDs—abstinence. The Medical

Institute for Sexual Health, P.O. Box 162306, Austin, TX 78716-2306. Phone: (800) 892-9484.

Abstinence Education Organizations and Programs

Abstinence Educators' Network (AEN)

AEN is a nonprofit organization of individuals and agencies who promote character-based/premarital abstinence education and support. AEN trains indigenous community leaders and local professionals (teachers, nurses, social workers, guidance counselors). A beginning course called "Foundations for Premarital Abstinence Education" and an advanced course called "Together We Can Reach Our Youth" are available. AEN provides a lending library and guest speakers for parent groups, schools, churches, and community agencies. Melanie Howell, P.O. Box 531, Mason, OH 45040. Phone: (513) 398-9801. E-mail: howeling@aol.com.

Best Friends

Best Friends is a mentoring program targeted specifically at girls in middle through high school. The program's success depends on the commitment level of the school guidance counselors or the mentors themselves. The Best Friends program focuses on abstinence and other issues that middle and high school girls face, such as self-esteem, relationships, career goals, and peer pressure. 4455 Connecticut Ave., N.W., Suite 310, Washington, D.C. 20008. Phone: (202) 822-9266; fax: (202) 822-9276.

Center for the 4th and 5th R's

Director Thomas Lickona is a nationally known speaker and author on character education and the importance of character in the area of sexuality education. Dr. Lickona, a behavioral psychologist and author of *Educating for Character*, is currently professor of education at State University of New York at Cortland. State University College at Cortland, P.O. Box 2000, Cortland, NY 13045.

Choices

Targeted at junior and senior high students in public and private schools, this program focuses on teen sexuality/abstinence. It also provides parents with information on sexual awareness. Presented in a classroom setting for five days, seminars are held locally in Orange, Los Angeles, and Riverside counties. 2545 East Chapman Avenue, Suite 220, Fullerton, CA 92831. Phone: (714) 525-5997; fax: (714) 525-5753. E-mail: waitfrsex@aol.com.

Creating Positive Relationships (CPR) Building Healthy Relationships
CPR is a not-for-profit organization dedicated to the growth of healthy relationships through the delivery of a unique curriculum for adolescents that promotes abstinence from sexual activity until marriage as the best choice in order to achieve optimal health for the individual and society. Linda Bartles, director, 30 North Rangeline Road, Suite A, Carmel, IN 46032. Phone: (317) 846-0386; fax: (317) 848-5055.

Crisis Pregnancy Centers of Greater Phoenix, Inc.
Prevention Services – TASk (Teens are Saying kNOw)
Prevention Services is a branch of the Crisis Pregnancy Centers of Greater Phoenix, Inc. TASk brings the freedoms-of-sexual-abstinence-until-marriage message to thousands of students. TASk programs are offered to school districts and organizations at no cost and provide trained teachers and program materials. TASk is composed of three distinct, tailor-made programs: middle school, high school, and college. Cynthia Cooper, 960 W. University, Suite 114, Tempe, AZ 85281. Phone: (602) 829-0707; fax: (602) 829-0458.

Carol Everett
Carol is an author and well-known speaker on abortion, sex education, and abstinence. She's a former abortion provider. Her story in the book *Bloody Money* is uplifting and eye-opening. P.O. Box 202463, Austin, TX 78720-2463. Phone: (512) 918-8060; fax: (512) 918-2810. E-mail: woman49@flash.net.

Lakita Garth
Lakita offers dynamic abstinence presentations to teens and "Gen X" audiences across the nation. She's a radio and television personality and former Miss Black California. Dominion Enterprises, P.O. Box 6107, Lakewood, CA 90714. Phone: (562) 429-0357.

Heritage Community Services

This nonprofit corporation provides educational and social services for schools, the military, and other American institutions. Services offered are from a community-wide, institution-wide perspective. Character and self-control programs are provided for public schools, the U.S. Navy, and sheriffs' offices, among others. Anne Badgley, Lowcounty Crisis Pregnancy Center, 2810 Ashley Phosphate, B-10, Charleston, SC 29418. Phone: (843) 863-0508; fax: (843) 863-0462.

Molly Kelly

Molly speaks nationally and internationally on the issue of teen abstinence. Geared to high school students, her presentations are both realistic and entertaining. As a widow and mother of eight, she takes speaking requests by mail so she can schedule her calendar. Videos, booklets, and a parent-teacher training manual can be ordered through the Center for Learning Corporation. 311 Roumfort Road, Philadelphia, PA 19119. Phone: (724) 964-8083. E-mail cfl@tratos/net. Web site: http://www.centerforlearning.org.

Project Reality

"Choosing the Best," a curriculum for junior and senior high students, is currently being piloted by Project Reality in 50 Illinois schools. The program combines components of *Sex, Lies &...the Truth,* 17 slides on STDs from the Medical Institute for Sexual Health, and parts of the *No Second Chance* video with Kathy Kay. P.O. Box 97, Golf, IL 60029-0097. Phone: (847) 729-3298; fax: (847) 729-9744. Web site: http://www.project-reality.pair.com.

Why kNOw

A community abstinence program designed to teach teens God's plan of waiting for marriage to have sex. 744 McCallie Ave., Suite 427, Chattanooga, TN 37403. Phone: (423) 267-8778; fax: (423) 267-7945. E-mail: mail@whyknow.org Web site: http://www.whyknow.org.

Worth Waiting For (WWF)
WWF is committed to the work of a God who redeems sin and poor choices and helps teens in their ongoing effort to sustain their decision for chastity. It provides professional counseling, teaching, training, mentoring programs, church education and support, and abstinence-till-marriage materials. Linda Klepacki and Dave Scherrer, P.O. Box 18888, Denver, CO 80218-0888. Phone: (888) 329-WAIT(9248).

RESOURCES FOR PARENTAL CHOICE CHAPTER

Education by Choice: The Case for Family Control, by John E. Coons and Stephen D.Sugarman (U. of California Press)
Coons and Sugarman were some of the first authors to make the case for choice on the basis of parental rights.

Schooling Christians: Holy Experiments in American Education, edited by Stanley Hauerwas and John H. Westerhoof (Eerdmans)
The three essays by Nicholas Wolterstorff, James Skillen, and Charles and Joshua Glenn present some of the important philosophical arguments for school choice.

The Myth of the Common School, by Charles Glenn (U. of Massachusetts Press)
The author, a leader in the educational reform movement, presents an historical overview of the idea that the state should sponsor popular education in order to mold common values among its citizens and, in turn, promote national unity. While examining some of the flaws of such a system within the framework of a democracy, Glenn also addresses a fundamental question: Who should control the education of a child, his parents or the state?

Disestablishment a Second Time: Genuine Pluralism for American Schools, by Rockne M. McCarthy, James Skillen, and William A. Harper (Eerdmans)
The authors analyze the public-education system in America and argue that to achieve justice among the variety of American worldviews, important structural changes in the funding of education must be made.

Private Vouchers, edited by Terry M. Moe (Hoover Institution Press)
Moe and others present empirical findings from the four major private voucher programs in existence. Of particular note is the preliminary finding that the programs do not increase social inequity and that disadvantaged populations reap substantial benefits.

The Closing of the American Heart, by Ronald H. Nash (Probe Ministries)
Nash contends that school choice would help solve some of the problems plaguing public schools. Furthermore, he contends that Christian schools need a higher vision for integrated Christian education.

Democracy and the Renewal of Public Education, edited by Richard John Neuhaus (Eerdmans)
Leading educators and educational analysts, including James Skillen, Rockne McCarthy, Charles Glenn, and Paul Vitz, address various problems in public education. The solutions they propose center on the fundamental necessity of school choice.

Religion and American Education: Rethinking a National Dilemma, by Warrem A. Nord (U. of North Carolina Press)
Nord presents compelling evidence that religious worldviews and perspectives are not presented or taken seriously in public education. Nord concludes, "If public school is as hostile to religion as I have suggested, then vouchers must be taken seriously."

The School Choice Controversy: What Is Constitutional? edited by James Skillen (Baker)
The essays in this volume address the legal questions associated with school choice proposals. Contributors include Richard Baer, Phillip Johnson, James Skillen, and Edward J. Larson.

Appendix D

VIDEO AND AUDIO RESOURCES

Teacher of the Year: (video geared toward teachers) Guy Doud presents a candid, affirming glimpse at the teaching profession; teachers draw strength and encouragement from Guy's inspiring story. Focus on the Family. (800) A-FAMILY. Also available is *What Dads Need to Know About Fathering* and *How to Raise the Strong-Willed Child*.

Preparing for Adolescence: An audio tape series for parents and children to listen to and discuss together, helping them to handle the pitfalls of adolescence. *How to Prepare for Adolescence*, a video for parents, offers concrete suggestions on how to help children avoid the identity crisis that leaves many young people feeling unloved and alienated. Focus on the Family. (800) A-FAMILY.

No Apologies: Focus on the Family's new sex education video. Focus on the Family. (800) A-FAMILY.

Masquerade: Focus on the Family's video for teens that explores candidly the harm done by alcohol and drug abuse, Focus on the Family. (800) A-FAMILY.

How Should We Then Live? and *Whatever Happened to the Human Race?*: Francis Schaeffer's video series on the history of Western Civilization.

Understanding the Times: A video curriculum which helps young people develop a Christian worldview, and prepares them for the Secular Humanist, Marxist, and New Age ideas they will be exposed to in colleges, universities, the business world, and through the media. Dr. David Nobel, Summit Ministries, P.O. Box 207, Manitou Springs, CO 80829. (719) 685-9103.

Appendix E

A CORE OF ESSENTIALS FOR THE WORKING PARENT

- Meet your child's teacher and principal at or before the beginning of school.
- Schedule a conference with the teacher within the first four weeks, as well as at each major marking period or semester. Although special times are sometimes scheduled for working parents, you may need to take off work for an hour for the conference. If an employer gives you trouble, you might suggest the old "ounce of prevention" time spent at a conference may mean less time off the job later if trouble should occur.
- Ask the teacher for "Grade Level Expectancies" for your child's grade, and a list of unit or monthly themes for classroom content.
- Be sure you see the work your child is doing and look at the papers returned to him; when classwork comes home, communicate with comments on it (to the teacher) to return. With a written note on the weekly work, encourage your child in some specific way or appreciate his efforts.
- Read the parent or school newsletters to stay informed about what's happening at school.
- Phone and/or send an occasional note to the teacher from work or home to thank her for her effort, to ask for help your child needs, or to offer help.
- Inform school personnel of your work schedule and how to reach you by phone during the school day. Make sure your child knows how to reach you at work.
- Express appreciation to the teacher sometime during the year.
- Plan with your child on a monthly calendar of school activities (like drama or musical programs your child is in, or night PTA meetings, school carnival, book fair, etc.), selecting and writing down the ones that are most important and that you can attend, given your work schedule (arrange to get videotape for others).
- Help your child set a time and place for homework, and provide support, materials, and encouragement.

- Have regular read-aloud times at home and listen to your child read (especially important for elementary age children).
- Consider a volunteer opportunity that you could coordinate with your work schedule, such as helping with a night fund-raiser, eating with your child and helping in the cafeteria one day a month, or taking one vacation day a year to help take the class on an outing.
- Share interesting happenings and elements of your work and life that relate to school activities.
- Talk to your company or employer about being a sponsor of your child's school.

If you let your child know that school is a very important place, that his education is a top priority to you, and that what he learns at school extends far beyond the classroom, you'll pave the way for an excellent education for him.

Appendix F

RELIGIOUS EXPRESSION IN PUBLIC SCHOOLS

In 1995, President Bill Clinton directed Secretary of Education Richard Riley to provide every school district in America with a statement of principles addressing religious expression in the public schools. The following is that information, which intended to clarify the First Amendment and rights of students, teachers, and parents:

"*Student prayer and religious discussion:* The Establishment Clause of the First Amendment does not prohibit purely private religious speech by students. Students therefore have the same right to engage in individual or group prayer and religious discussions during the school day as they do to engage in other comparable activity. For example, students may read their Bibles or other scriptures, say grace before meals, and pray before tests to the same extent they may engage in comparable non-disruptive activities. Local school authorities possess substantial discretion to impose rules of order and other pedagogical restrictions on student activities, but they may not structure or administer such rules to discriminate against religious activity or speech.

"Generally, students may pray in a nondisruptive manner when not engaged in school activities or instruction, and subject to the rules that normally pertain in the applicable setting. Specifically, students in informal settings, such as cafeterias and hallways, may pray and discuss their religious views with each other, subject to the same rules of order as apply to other student activities and speech. Students may also speak to, and attempt to persuade, their peers about religious topics just as they do with regard to political topics. School officials, however, should intercede to stop student speech that constitutes harassment aimed at a student or a group of students.

"Students may also participate in before or after school events with religious content, such as 'see you at the flag pole' gatherings, on the same terms as they may participate in other noncurriculum activities on school premises. School officials may neither discourage nor encourage participation in such an event.

"The right to engage in voluntary prayer or religious discussion free from discrimination does not include the right to have a captive audience listen, or to compel other students to participate. Teachers and school administrators should ensure that no student is in any way coerced to participate in religious activity.

"*Graduation prayer and baccalaureates:* Under current Supreme Court decisions, school officials may not mandate or organize prayer at graduation, nor organize religious baccalaureate ceremonies. If a school generally opens its facilities to private groups, it must make its facilities available on the same terms to organizers of privately sponsored religious baccalaureate services. A school may not extend preferential treatment to baccalaureate ceremonies and may in some instances be obliged to disclaim official endorsement of such ceremonies.

"*Official neutrality regarding religious activity:* Teachers and school administrators, when acting in those capacities, are representatives of the state and are prohibited by the establishment clause from soliciting or encouraging religious activity, and from participating in such activity with students. Teachers and administrators also are prohibited from discouraging activity because of its religious content, and from soliciting or encouraging antireligious activity.

"*Teaching about religion:* Public schools may not provide religious instruction, but they may teach *about* religion, including the Bible or other scripture: the history of religion, comparative religion, the Bible (or other scripture) as literature, and the role of religion in the history of the United States and other countries all are permissible public school subjects. Similarly, it is permissible to consider religious influences on art, music, literature, and social studies. Although public schools may teach about religious holidays, including their religious aspects, and may celebrate the secular aspects of holidays, schools may not observe holidays as religious events or promote such observance by students.

"*Student assignments:* Students may express their beliefs about religion in the form of homework, artwork, and other written and oral assignments free of discrimination based on the religious content of their submissions. Such home and classroom work should be judged by ordinary academic standards of substance and relevance, and against other legitimate pedagogical concerns identified by the school.

"*Religious literature:* Students have a right to distribute religious literature to their schoolmates on the same terms as they are permitted to distribute other literature that is unrelated to school curriculum or activities. Schools may impose the same reasonable time, place, and manner or other constitutional restrictions on distribution of religious literature as they do on nonschool literature generally, but they may not single out religious literature for special regulation.

"*Religious excusals:* Subject to applicable State laws, schools enjoy substantial discretion to excuse individual students from lessons that are objectionable to the student or the students' parents on religious or other conscientious grounds. School officials may neither encourage nor discourage students from availing themselves of an excusal option. Under the Religious Freedom Restoration Act, if it is proved that particular lessons substantially burden a student's free exercise of religion and if the school cannot prove a compelling interest in requiring attendance, the school would be legally required to excuse the student.

"*Released time:* Subject to applicable State laws, schools have the discretion to dismiss students to off-premises religious instruction, provided that schools do not encourage or discourage participation or penalize those who do not attend. Schools may not allow religious instruction by outsiders on school premises during the school day.

"*Teaching values:* Though schools must be neutral with respect to religion, they may play an active role with respect to teaching civic values and virtue, and the moral code that holds us together as a community. The fact that some of these values are held also by religions does not make it unlawful to teach them in school.

"*Student garb:* Students may display religious messages on items of clothing to the same extent that they are permitted to display other comparable messages. Religious messages may not be singled out for suppression, but rather are subject to the same rules as generally apply to comparable messages. When wearing particular attire, such as yarmulkes and headscarves, during the school day is part of students' religious practice, under the Religious Freedom Restoration Act schools generally may not prohibit the wearing of such items.

"The Equal Access Act

"The Equal Access Act is designed to ensure that, consistent with the First Amendment, student religious activities are accorded the same access to public school facilities as are student secular activities. Based on decisions of the Federal courts, as well as its interpretations of the Act, the Department of Justice has advised that the Act should be interpreted as providing, among other things, that:

"*General provisions:* Student religious groups at public secondary schools have the same right of access to school facilities as is enjoyed by other comparable student groups. Under the Equal Access Act, a school receiving Federal funds that allows one or more student noncurriculum-related clubs to meet on its premises during noninstructional time may not refuse access to student religious groups.

"*Prayer services and worship exercises covered:* A meeting, as defined and protected by the Equal Access Act, may include a prayer service, Bible reading, or other worship exercise.

"*Equal access to means of publicizing meetings:* A school receiving Federal funds must allow student groups meeting under the Act to use the school media—including the public address system, the school newspaper, and the school bulletin board—to announce their meetings on the same terms as other noncurriculum-related student groups are allowed to use the school media. Any policy concerning the use of school media must be applied to all noncurriculum-related student groups in a nondiscriminatory manner. Schools, however, may inform students that certain groups are not school sponsored.

"*Lunchtime and recess covered:* A school creates a limited open forum under the Equal Access Act, triggering equal access rights for religious groups, when it allows students to meet during their lunch periods or other noninstructional time during the school day, as well as when it allows students to meet before and after the school day."

(Richard Riley, U.S. Dept. of Education, August 10, 1995)

Appendix G

STUDENTS' BILL OF RIGHTS ON A PUBLIC SCHOOL CAMPUS

I. THE RIGHT to Meet with Other Religious Students.

The *Equal Access Act* allows students the freedom to meet on campus for the purpose of discussing religious issues.

II. THE RIGHT to Identify Your Religious Beliefs Through Signs and Symbols.

Students are free to express their religious beliefs through signs and symbols.

III. THE RIGHT to Talk About Your Religious Beliefs on Campus.

Freedom of speech is a fundamental right mandated in the Constitution and does not exclude the school yard.

IV. THE RIGHT to Distribute Religious Literature on Campus.

Distributing literature on campus may not be restricted simply because it is religious.

V. THE RIGHT to Pray on Campus.

Students may pray alone or with others so long as it does not disrupt school activities or is not forced on others.

VI. THE RIGHT to Carry or Study Your Bible on Campus.

The Supreme Court has said that only *state-directed* Bible reading is unconstitutional.

VII. THE RIGHT to Do Research Papers, Speeches, and Creative Projects With Religious Themes.

The First Amendment does not forbid all mention of religion in public schools.

VIII. THE RIGHT to Be Exempt.

Students may be exempt from activities and class content that contradict their religious beliefs.

IX. THE RIGHT to Celebrate or Study Religious Holidays on Campus.

Music, art, literature, and drama that have religious themes are permitted as part of the curriculum for school activities if presented in an objective manner as a traditional part of the cultural and religious heritage of the particular holiday.

X. THE RIGHT to Meet with School Officials.

The First Amendment to the Constitution forbids Congress to make any law that would restrict the right of the people to petition the government (school officials).

 The book *Students' Legal Rights on a Public School Campus* (detailing each right) may be obtained by calling or writing Roever Communications, P.O. Box 136130, Ft. Worth, TX 76136. (817) 238-2000.

Appendix H

QUESTIONS TO ASK SCHOOL BOARD CANDIDATES

1. What do you think is the most pressing issue facing our schools today?
2. As a general principle do you believe that books containing sexually explicit material or sexually deviant material should be available in:
   a. elementary school libraries?
   b. junior high school libraries?
   c. senior high school libraries?
   d. public libraries?
3. Do you believe in unrestricted academic freedom which would allow for anything in print being available in categories listed above?
4. Do you believe the local school board should have the final say concerning the quality and content of curriculum?
5. Do you believe parents should serve on curriculum committees?
6. Should an AIDS education program promote abstinence as the primary protection from the HIV/AIDS virus or promote "safer sex" with condoms?
7. Would you be willing to incorporate into your AIDS program curriculum that would teach refusal skills and reasons to say "no" to sex and drugs?
8. Do you view the superintendent as an administrator over the board, or as an administrator hired by the board?
9. As a spokesperson on the board, list who you would be representing, in order of priority:
   a. superintendent
   b. taxpayers/parents
   c. teachers
10. Do you believe parents in the school district have a right to call a board member with their concerns? Would you be open to parents calling you with their concerns?
11. Do you believe sex education classes should begin at kindergarten? If not, at what grade level?

12. Do you believe in mandatory sex education or by parent permission only?
13. Were you asked to run for school board? If yes, by whom? Why did you decide to run?
14. Do you believe that parents have the highest investment in the schools and therefore the administration should respond to their concerns?
15. Should taxpayers have more input into the school budget?
16. Do you support "educational choice plans" for public schools, in which a student could choose to attend the school of his or her choice within a district or state?
17. Would you encourage parents to have less say or more say in their children's curricula and library books?
18. Do you support an "open door policy" and "equal access" for religious groups in the public schools, such as a student-sponsored Bible study as an extra-curricular activity?
19. Do you have relatives who work in the school system in which you are running for office?
20. Do you believe in merit pay for teachers?
21. Please describe in your own words what you know about Planned Parenthood's family life sexuality education comprehensive program.
22. Would you be in favor of Planned Parenthood making presentations in the classroom?
23. Do you support the teaching of homosexuality as an acceptable alternative lifestyle?
24. Where does most of your financial support come from?
    a. special interest groups
    b. teachers' union
    c. community donations
    d. other

Reprinted with permission from *The Parent's Right to Know* by Wendy Flint, Vancouver, WA, 1990, p. 50.

Appendix I

CAN'T-MISS TREASURES: A SUPPLEMENTAL HOME READING LIST

Here is a sampling of classics to read to and with children which form a solid background for excellent language development and comprehension, appreciation of fine literature, and a wide vocabulary. Many of these books children will not encounter in school. There are books in this list covering a wide range of interests, cultures, and periods. As you read together, you give your child an opportunity to sample many different styles in order to develop his own favorite authors and topics.

If children in primary years are not given the opportunity of reading classic literature, they will be unprepared and disinterested in the classics when they encounter them in their secondary education. Most of these selections should be read to children before they can actually read them themselves, with the parent explaining historical background or language so the child can understand the story. Remember that children are able to listen and comprehend material *far above their ability* to read it. As they get older and advance in reading skills, you can read some selections aloud together and your teen can read some independently.

This list is not exhaustive—it's only a beginning; great for summer reading, for choosing book reports, for travel and rainy day reading. You can add your favorites as you develop your own family library and as your child's reading tastes develop:

Primary Grades

Preschool

Bemelmens, Ludwig—*Madeline*
Brown, Margaret Wise—*Good Night, Moon*
Burton, Virginia Lee—*Mike Mulligan and His Steam Shovel, The Real Mother Goose*

Dalgliesh, Alice—*The Bears on Hemlock Mountain*, *The Courage of Sarah Noble*
Freeman, Don—*Cordoroy*
McCloskey, Robert—*Make Way for Ducklings*, *Blueberries for Sal*
Milne, A. A.—*When We Were Very Young* books on
    Christopher Robin, *Winnie the Pooh*, *The House at Pooh Corner*
Piper, Watty—*Little Engine that Could*, *Mother Goose*, *A Treasury of Best*
    Loved Rhymes
Potter, Beatrix—*The Tales of Peter Rabbit* series
Slobodkin, Esphyr—*Caps for Sale*
Stevenson, Robert Louis—*A Child's Garden of Verses*
Ward, Lynd—*Biggest Bear*

Elementary

Atwater, Richard and Florence—*Mr. Popper's Penguins*
Barrie, James M.—*Peter Pan*
Baum, L. Frank—*The Wizard of Oz*
Bond, Michael—*Paddington*
Brink, Carol Ryrie—*Caddie Woodlawn*
Burnett, Frances Hodgson—*The Secret Garden*, *A Little Princess*
D'Aulaire, Ingri and Perin—*George Washington*, *Abraham*, *Lincoln*
Dalgliesh, Alice—*The Bears on Hemlock Mountain*
Daughtery, James—*Landing of the Pilgrims*
Dodge, Mary Mapes—*Hans Brinker and the Silver Skates*
Enright, Elizabeth—*Thimble Summer*
Farley, Walter—*The Black Stallion* series
Forbes, Esther—*Johnny Tremain*
Grahame, Kenneth—*Wind in the Willows*
Green, Norma—*The Hole in the Dike*, retold
Henry, Marguerite—*Justin Morgan Had a Horse*, *Brighty of Grand Canyon*,
    Misty of Chincoteague
Hunt, Irene—*Across Five Aprils*
Kipling, Rudyard—*Just So Stories*, *The Jungle Books*
Kjelgard, Jim—*Big Red*
L'Engle, Madeline—*A Wrinkle in Time*
Lawson, Robert—*Pilgrim's Progress* adaptation

Lewis, C. S.—*Chronicles of Narnia: The Lion, the Witch and the Wardrobe, Prince Caspian, The Voyage of the Dawn Treader, The Silver Chair, The Horse & His Boy, The Magician's Nephew, The Last Battle*
Lorenzini, Carlo—*Pinocchio*
MacDonald, George—*The Princess and the Goblin, The Princess and the Curdie, The Gifts of the Christ Child, Fairy Tales and Stories for the Childlike*
Rawls, Wilson—*Where the Red Fern Grows*
Sandburg, Carl—*Abe Lincoln Grows Up*
Sewell, Anna—*Black Beauty*
Sidney, Margaret—*Five Little Peppers and How They Grew*
Speare, Elizabeth George—*Calico Captive*
Spyri, Johanna—*Heidi*
Stevenson, Robert Louis—*A Child's Garden of Verses, Treasure Island*
Taylor, Sidney—*All of a Kind Family*
White, E. B.—*Charlotte's Web, The Trumpet of the Swan, Stuart Little*
Wiggin, Kate Douglas—*Rebecca of Sunnybrook Farm*
Wilder, Laura Ingles—*Little House* series
Williams, Margery—*Velveteen Rabbit*
Guinness Book of World Records (not a classic, but almost any child loves to read about the tallest person in the world, the fastest person, and other amazing records)

Secondary Grades

Adams, Richard—*Watership Down*
Alcott, Louisa May—*Little Women, Little Men, Jo's Boys*
Austen, Jane—*Pride and Prejudice*
Bronte, Charlotte—*Jane Eyre*
Bronte, Emily—*Wuthering Heights*
Bunyan, John—*Pilgrim's Progress*
Carroll, Lewis—*Alice in Wonderland, Through the Looking Glass*
Collum, Padraic—*Children's Homer, Adventures of Odysseus* and the *Tale of Troy* based on Homer's Iliad and Odyssey, retold by Padraic Collum
Cooper, James Fenimore—*The Last of the Mohicans*

Defoe, Daniel—*Robinson Crusoe*, *The Farther Adventures of Robinson Crusoe*

Dickens, Charles—*A Tale of Two Cities*, *Oliver Twist*, *David Copperfield*

Frost, Robert—*You Come Too*

Gilbreath, Frank—*Cheaper by the Dozen*

Gipson, Fred—*Old Yeller*

Herriott, James—*All Creatures Great and Small* series

Keith, Harold—*Rifles for Watie*

Kipling, Rudyard—*Kim*

Knight, Eric—*Lassie, Come Home*

Lewis, C. S.—*A Space Trilogy*

Meigs, Cornelia—*Invincible Louisa* (not a classic, but a wonderful biography of Louisa May Alcott)

Montgomery, L. M.—*Anne of Green Gables* series: *Anne of Avonlea*, *Anne of the Island*, *Anne of Ingleside*, *Anne's House of Dreams*, *Anne of Windy Poplars*

Rawlings, Marjorie Kennon—*The Yearling*

Scott, Sir Walter—*Ivanhoe*

Sewell, Anna—*Black Beauty*

Shakespeare, William—*The Taming of the Shrew*, *Hamlet*, *A Midsummer Night's Dream* (Shakespeare is interesting even at a young age, especially if children can see it performed at a local college or community theater.)

Speare, Elizabeth Georg—*The Bronze Bow*

Stevenson, Robert Louis—*Kidnapped*, *Treasure Island*

Swift, Jonathan—*Gulliver's Travels*

Tolkien, J.R.R.—*The Hobbit*, *The Lord of the Rings*

Twain, Mark—*The Adventures of Huckleberry Finn*, *Tom Sawyer*, *A Connecticut Yankee in King Arthur's Court*, *The Prince and the Pauper*

Verne, Jules—*Around the World in Eighty Days*, *Voyage to the Bottom of the Sea*

Wallace, Lew—*Ben-Hur*

My thanks to Susan Gaines for her outstanding contribution to the Home Reading List and her love of books and children.

ALSO BY CHERI FULLER

Through the Learning Glass: A Child's Nine Learning Windows You Don't Want to Miss
When Families Pray
When Children Pray
When Mothers Pray
Extraordinary Kids: Nurturing and Championing Your Child with Special Needs
Quiet Whispers from God's Heart for Women
Trading Your Worry for Wonder
21 Days to Helping Your Child Learn
Teaching Your Child to Write
Motherhood 101
Christmas Treasures of the Heart
Unlocking Your Child's Learning Potential
365 Ways to Develop Your Child's Values
365 Ways to Build Your Child's Self-Esteem
365 Ways to Help Your Child Learn
How to Grow a Young Music Lover
Home Business Happiness

Cheri Fuller is a mother of three grown children, a grandmother, and a former teacher who has worked with kids at every level, from elementary school to high school and college. She's also a contributing editor for *Today's Christian Woman* and a writer whose articles have appeared in magazines such as *Focus on the Family*, *Family Circle*, *CHILD*, and *ParentLife*. A dynamic, motivational speaker, Cheri loves inspiring others as she speaks at women's retreats and parent conferences around the country.

You can contact Cheri at:
P.O. Box 770493
Oklahoma City, OK 73177
Fax: (405) 749-1381. E-mail: cheri@cander.net
You can also visit her Web site at www.CheriFuller.com.

Other Books to Strengthen Your Relationships

From Focus on the Family®

The Way They Learn

Make the most of your kids' schooling by understanding *The Way They Learn.* By defining a wide variety of learning styles, educational specialist and author Cynthia Ulrich Tobias reveals the ways you can use each child's natural strengths and interests to boost their academic achievement. Frustration surrounding study habits often results from a mismatch in learning styles—yours and theirs. But with the practical approaches found in this paperback, you'll soon be "speaking your kids' individual languages" and stimulating their learning in ways you never imagined.

Extraordinary Kids

Most parents expect their babies to be born physically and mentally perfect. And while the vast majority are, a special few are not. *Extraordinary Kids* gives mothers and fathers the hope, inspiration, and insight needed to nurture and champion a special-needs child. Learn from Cheri Fuller, an educator and author, and Louise Tucker Jones, a mother who's successfully raised a Down syndrome youngster. Includes everything from handling grief to finding a support network. Paperback.

Every Child Can Succeed

Bring out the success in your child! Every child receives, processes, and uses information differently. Discovering a child's unique style can affect how well he or she does in school, at work—even in life. Educational specialist Cynthia Ulrich Tobias has more to say on the subject of learning styles in *Every Child Can Succeed.* Who's to say you won't unlock another Einstein or Picasso living at your house?! Paperback

• • •

Look for these special books in your Christian bookstore, or request a copy by calling 1-800-A-FAMILY (1-800-232-6459). Friends in Canada may write Focus on the Family, P.O. Box 9800, Stn. Terminal, Vancouver, B.C. V6B 4G3 or call 1-800-661-9800.

Visit our Web site (www.family.org) to learn more about the ministry or find out if there is a Focus on the Family office in your country.

FOCUS ON THE FAMILY®

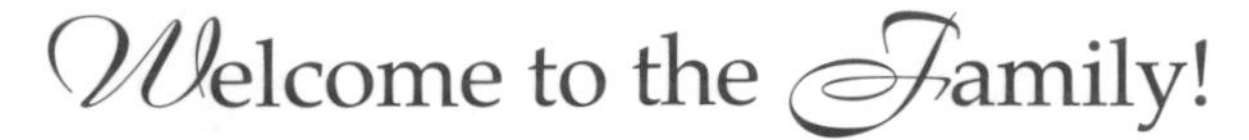

Whether you received this book as a gift, borrowed it from a friend, or purchased it yourself, we're glad you read it! It's just one of the many helpful, insightful, and encouraging resources produced by Focus on the Family.

In fact, that's what Focus on the Family is all about—providing inspiration, information, and biblically based advice to people in all stages of life.

It began in 1977 with the vision of one man, Dr. James Dobson, a licensed psychologist and author of 16 best-selling books on marriage, parenting, and family. Alarmed by the societal, political, and economic pressures that were threatening the existence of the American family, Dr. Dobson founded Focus on the Family with one employee—an assistant—and a once-a-week radio broadcast, aired on only 36 stations.

Now an international organization, Focus on the Family is dedicated to preserving Judeo-Christian values and strengthening the family through more than 70 different ministries, including eight separate daily radio broadcasts; television public service announcements; 11 publications; and a steady series of award-winning books, films, and videos for people of all ages and interests.

Recognizing the needs of, as well as the sacrifices and important contribution made by, such diverse groups as educators, physicians, attorneys, crisis pregnancy center staff, and single parents, Focus on the Family offers specific outreaches to uphold and minister to these individuals, too. And it's all done for one purpose, and one purpose only: to encourage and strengthen individuals and families through the life-changing message of Jesus Christ.

• • •

For more information about the ministry, or if we can be of help to your family, simply write to Focus on the Family, Colorado Springs, CO 80995 or call 1-800-A-FAMILY (1-800-232-6459). Friends in Canada may write Focus on the Family, P.O. Box 9800, Stn. Terminal, Vancouver, B.C. V6B 4G3 or call 1-800-661-9800. Visit our Web site—www.family.org—to learn more about the ministry or to find out if there is a Focus on the Family office in your country.

We'd love to hear from you!